LEARN GERMAN WITH LITERATURE:

IMMENSEE BY THEODOR STORM

ISBN: 978-1-988830-65-0

This book is published by Bermuda Word. It has been created with specialized software that produces a three line interlinear format.

Please contact us if you would like a version with different font, font size, or font colors and/or less words per page!

LEARN-TO-READ-FOREIGN-LANGUAGES.COM

Dear Reader and Language Learner!

You're reading the Paperback edition of Bermuda Word's interlinear and pop-up HypLern Reader App. Before you start reading German, please read this explanation of our method.

Since we want you to read German and to learn German, our method consists primarily of word-for-word literal translations, but we add idiomatic German if this helps understanding the sentence.

For example:
Er fing   von neuem an zu schreien.
He caught from new   on to scream
[He started to scream again.]

The HypLern method entails that you re-read the text until you know the high frequency words just by reading, and then mark and learn the low frequency words separately or practice them with our brilliant App.

Don't forget to take a look at the e-book App with integrated learning software at learn-to-read-foreign-languages.com!

Thanks for your patience and enjoy the story and learning German!

LEARN-TO-READ-FOREIGN-LANGUAGES.COM

Table of Contents

Der Alte

Der	Alte
The	Old (one)

An	einem	Spätherbstnachmittage	ging	ein	alter
On	a	late autumn afternoon	went	an	old

wohlgekleideter	Mann	langsam	die	Straße	hinab.	Er
well dressed	man	slowly	the	street	to-down (down)	He

schien	von	einem	Spaziergange	nach	Hause
seemed	from	a	walk	to	house home

zurückzukehren,	denn	seine	Schnallenschuhe,	die	einer
turn back	since	his	laced shoes	which	a

vorübergegangenen	Mode	angehörten,	waren	bestäubt.
over-passed (outdated)	fashion	belonged	were	dusty

Den	langen	Rohrstock	mit	goldenem	Knopf	trug	er
The	long	cane	with	(a) golden	button	carried	he

unter	dem	Arm;	mit	seinen	dunklen	Augen,	in	welche
under	the	arm	with	his	dark	eyes	in	which

sich	die	ganze	verlorene	Jugend	gerettet	zu	haben
themselves	the	total	lost	youth	rescued	to	have

schien,	und	welche	eigentümlich	von	den	schneeweißen
seemed	and	which	curiously	from	the	snow-white

Haaren	abstachen,	sah	er	ruhig	umher	oder	in	die
hair	stuck off	looked	he	calmly	around	or	in	the

Stadt	hinab,	welche	im	Abendsonnendufte	vor	ihm
city	to-down (down)	which	in the	evening-sun-fragrance	before	him

lag.
lay

Er	schien	fast	ein	Fremder,	denn	von	den
He	seemed	almost	a	stranger	since	from	the

Vorübergehenden	grüßten	ihn	nur	wenige,	obgleich
passer-by	greeted	him	only	few	although

mancher	unwillkürlich	in	diese	ernsten	Augen	zu	sehen
many	involuntarily	in	these	serious	eyes	to	see

gezwungen	wurde.
forced	were

Endlich	stand	er	vor	einem	hohen	Giebelhause	still,
Finally	stood	he	before	a	large	gable-home	~~quiet~~

sah	noch	einmal	in	die	Stadt	hinaus	und	trat	dann
saw	still	once	in	the	city	out	and	stepped	then

in	die	Hausdiele.	Bei	dem	Schall	der	Türglocke	wurde
in	the	house-hall	By	it	sounded	the	doorbell	became

drinnen	in	der	Stube	von	einem	Guckfenster,	welches
inside	in	the	room	from	a	peering window	which

nach	der	Diele	hinausging,	der	grüne	Vorhang
behind	the	hall	went out	the	green	curtain

weggeschoben	und	das	Gesicht	einer	alten	Frau
away	and	the	face	of an	old	woman

2

dahinter sichtbar. Der Mann winkte ihr mit seinem
there behind visible The man waved her with his

Rohrstock.
cane

"Noch kein Licht!" sagte er in einem etwas südlichen
Still no light said he in a somewhat southern

Akzent, und die Haushälterin ließ den Vorhang wieder
accent and the female housekeeper let the curtain again

fallen.
fall

Der Alte ging nun über die weite Hausdiele, durch
The old one went now over the wide house hall through

einen Pesel, wo große eichene Schränke mit
a living room where large oaken cupboards with

Porzellanvasen an den Wänden standen; durch die
china vases by the windows stood through the

gegenüberstehende Tür trat er in einen kleinen Flur,
opposite standing door stepped he in a small floor

von wo aus eine enge Treppe zu den obern
from where out a narrow stairs to the upper

Zimmern des Hinterhauses führte. Er stieg sie
rooms of the back house led He rose (climbed) them

3

langsam	hinauf,	schloß	oben	eine	Tür	auf	und	trat
slowly	up	locked (opened)	upstairs	a	door	up	and	stepped

dann	in	ein	mäßig	großes	Zimmer.
then	in	a	moderately	large	room

Hier	war	es	heimlich	und	still;	die	eine	Wand	war
Here	was	it	private	and	quiet	the	one	wall	was

fast	mit	Repositorien	und	Bücherschränken	bedeckt,	an
almost	with	repoitories	and	bookcases	covered	by

den	andern	hingen	Bilder	von	Menschen	und	Gegenden;
the	others	hung	images	from	people	and	areas

vor	einem	Tisch	mit	grüner	Decke,	auf	dem	einzelne
before	a	table	with	green	cover	on	which	single

aufgeschlagene	Bücher	umherlagen,	stand	ein
up-struck (opened)	books	lay around	stood	a

schwerfälliger	Lehnstuhl	mit	rotem	Samtkissen.
heavy	lean-chair (armchair)	with	red	velvet cushion

Nachdem	der	Alte	Hut	und	Stock	in	die	Ecke	gestellt
After	the	old	hat	and	stick	in	the	corner	set

hatte,	setzte	er	sich	in	den	Lehnstuhl	und	schien	mit
had	set	he	himself	in	the	lean-chair (armchair)	and	seemed	with

gefalteten	Händen	von	seinem	Spaziergange	auszuruhen.
folded	hands	from	his	walk	out-to-rest

Wie	er	so	saß,	wurde	es	allmählich	dunkler;	endlich
As	he	so	sat	became	it	gradually	more dark	finally

4

fiel ein Mondstrahl durch die Fensterscheiben auf die
fell a moon-beam through the window-panes on the

Gemälde an der Wand, und wie der helle Streif
painting on the wall and as the bright stripe

langsam weiter rückte, folgten die Augen des Mannes
slowly farther moved followed the eyes of the man

unwillkürlich.
involuntarily

Nun trat er über ein kleines Bild in schlichtem
Now stepped he over a small image in simple

schwarzem Rahmen. "Elisabeth!" sagte der Alte leise;
black frame Elisabeth said the old slowly

und wie er das Wort gesprochen, war die Zeit
and as he the word spoke was the time

verwandelt: er war in seiner Jugend.
changed he was in his youth

Die Kinder

Die Kinder
The kids

Bald trat die anmutige Gestalt eines kleinen
Soon stepped the graceful shape of a little

Mädchens zu ihm. Sie hieß Elisabeth und
girl to him. She was called Elisabeth and

mochte fünf Jahre er selbst war doppelt so alt.
might five years he himself was double so old
zählen,
count
was five years old

Um den Hals trug sie ein rotseidenes Tüchelchen;
Around the neck carried she a red-silken little cloth
(wore)

das ließ ihr hübsch zu den braunen Augen.
that let her handsome to the brown eyes
(went)

"Reinhard!" rief sie, "wir haben frei, frei! den
Reinhard called she (out) we have free free the
(are)

ganzen Tag keine Schule, und morgen auch nicht."
whole day no school and tomorrow also not

Reinhard stellte die Rechentafel, die er schon unterm
Reinhard set the calculation-table that he already under the
(abacus)

Arm hatte, flink hinter die Haustür, und dann liefen
arm had quickly behind the house door and then ran

6

beide	Kinder	durchs	Haus	in	den	Garten	und	durch
both	children	through the	house	in	the	garden	and	through

die	Gartenpforte	hinaus	auf	die	Wiese.	Die	unverhofften
the	garden door	to-out (outside)	on	the	meadow	The	unexpected

Ferien	kamen	ihnen	herrlich	zustatten.
vacation	came	them	wonderfully	to stead
		were wonderful to them		

Reinhard	hatte	hier	mit	Elisabeths	Hilfe	ein	Haus	aus
Reinhard	had	here	with	Elisabeth's	help	a	house	from

Rasenstücken	aufgeführt;	darin	wollten	sie	die
turf-pieces	erected	there-in	wanted	they	the

Sommerabende	wohnen;	aber	es	fehlte	noch	die	Bank.
summer evenings	live	but	it	lacked	still	the	bench

Nun	ging	er	gleich	an	die	Arbeit;	Nägel,	Hammer
Now	went	he	immediately	to	~~the~~	work	nails	hammer

und	die	nötigen	Bretter	waren	schon	bereit.
and	the	necessary	boards	were	already	ready

Während	dessen	ging	Elisabeth	an	dem	Wall	entlang
While	this	went	Elisabeth	to	the	wall	by
Meanwhile						along the wall	

und	sammelte	den	ringförmigen	Samen	der	wilden
and	gathered	the	ring-formed	seed	of the	wild

Malve	in	ihre	Schürze;	davon	wollte	sie	sich	Ketten
mallow	in	her	apron	there from	wanted	she	herself	chains

und	Halsbänder	machen;	und	als	Reinhard	endlich	trotz
and	neck-bands	make	and	as	Reinhard	finally	despite

7

manches	krumm	geschlagenen	Nagels	seine	Bank
many	crooked	hit	nail	hit	bench

dennoch	zustande	gebracht	hatte	und	nun	wieder	in
then yet	to-stand	brought finished	had	and	now	again	in

die	Sonne	hinaustrat,	ging	sie	schon	weit	davon	am
the	sun	came out	went	she	already	far	there-from	to the

andern	Ende	der	Wiese.
other	end	of the	meadow

"Elisabeth!"	rief	er,	"Elisabeth!"	und	da	kam	sie,
Elisabeth	called	he (out)	Elisabeth	and	there	came	she

und	ihre	Locken	flogen.
and	her	curls	flew

"Komm,"	sagte	er,	"nun	ist	unser	Haus	fertig.	Du	bist
Come	said	he	now	is	our	house	ready	You	are (have)

ja	ganz	heiß	geworden;	komm	herein,	wir	wollen	uns
well	all	hot	become	come	inside	we	want	us

auf	die	neue	Bank	setzen.	Ich	erzähl'	dir	etwas."
on	the	new	bench	set	I	(will) tell	you	something

Dann	gingen	sie	beide	hinein	und	setzten	sich	auf
Then	went	they	both	inside	and	set	themselves	on

die	neue	Bank.	Elisabeth	nahm	ihre	Ringelchen	aus	der
the	new	bench	Elisabeth	took	her	little rings	from	her

Schürze	und	zog	sie	auf	lange	Bindfäden;	Reinhard
apron	and	pulled (strung)	them	on	long	threads	Reinhard

8

| fing | an | zu | erzählen: | "Es | waren | einmal | drei |
| caught on / started | | to | tell | There | were | one time | three |

Spinnfrauen..."
spin women

| "Ach," | sagte | Elisabeth, | "das | weiß | ich | ja | auswendig; | du |
| Ah | said | Elisabeth | that | know | I | yes | by heart | you |

| mußt | auch | nicht | immer | dasselbe | erzählen." |
| must | also | not | always | the same | tell |

| Da | mußte | Reinhard | die | Geschichte | von | den | drei |
| Then | must | Reinhard | the | story | of | the | three |

| Spinnfrauen | stecken | lassen, | und | statt | dessen | erzählte |
| spin women | stick (go) | let | and | instead | of that | told |

| er | die | Geschichte | von | dem | armen | Mann, | der | in | die |
| he | the | story | of | the | poor | man | who | in | the |

| Löwengrube | geworfen | war. |
| lion's den | thrown | was |

| "Nun | war | es | Nacht," | sagte | er, | "weißt | du? | ganz |
| Now | was | it | night | said | he | know | you | all |

| finstere, | und | die | Löwen | schliefen. | Mitunter | aber |
| dark | and | the | lions | slept | Middle-under (Meanwhile) | however |

| gähnten | sie | im | Schlaf | und | reckten | die | roten | Zungen |
| yawned | they | in the | sleep | and | stretched | the | red | tongues |

| aus; | dann | schauderte | der | Mann | und | meinte, | daß | der |
| out | then | shivered | the | man | and | believed | that | the |

9

Morgen komme. Da warf es um ihn her auf einmal
morning came Then threw it around him to at once
there around him

einen hellen Schein, und als er aufsah, stand ein
a bright shine and when he looked up stood an

Engel vor ihm. Der winkte ihm mit der Hand und
angel before him This one waved him with the hand and

ging dann gerade in die Felsen hinein."
went then straight in the rocks inside

Elisabeth hatte aufmerksam zugehört. "Ein Engel?" sagte
Elisabeth had attentively listened An angel said

sie: "Hatte er denn Flügel?"
she Had he then wings

"Es ist nur so eine Geschichte," antwortete Reinhard;
It is just so a story answered Reinhard

"es gibt ja gar keine Engel."
it gives yes indeed no angels
there are

"O pfui, Reinhard!" sagte sie und sah ihm starr ins
Oh pfew Reinhard said she and saw him rigid in the

Gesicht.
face

10

Als er sie aber finster anblickte, fragte sie ihn
When he her however dark stared at asked she him

zweifelnd: "Warum sagen sie es denn immer? Mutter
doubting Why say they it then always Mother

und Tante und auch in der Schule?"
and aunt and also in the school

"Das weiß ich nicht," antwortete er.
That know I not answered he

"Aber du," sagte Elisabeth, "gibt es denn auch keine
But you said Elisabeth gives it then also no
exist

Löwen?"
lions

"Löwen? Ob es Löwen gibt? In Indien; da spannen
Lions If it lions gives In India there hitch
lions exist

die Götzenpriester sie vor den Wagen und fahren
the idolatrous priests them before the cart and drive

mit ihnen durch die Wüste. Wenn ich groß bin, will
with them through the desert When I large am want
(grown up)

ich einmal selber hin. Da ist es viel tausendmal
I once (my)self (there) to There is it many thousand time(s)

schöner als hier bei uns; da gibt es gar keinen
more beautiful as here with us there gives it at all no
is

Winter. Du mußt auch mit mir. Willst du?"
winter You must also (along) with me Want you
Do you want to

11

"Ja," sagte Elisabeth; "aber Mutter muß dann auch mit,
Yes said Elisabeth but mother must then also along

und deine Mutter auch."
and your mother also

"Nein," sagte Reinhard, "die sind dann zu alt, die
No said Reinhard they are then too old they

können nicht mit."
can not (go) along

"Ich darf aber nicht allein."
I dare however not alone

"Du sollst schon dürfen; du wirst dann wirklich
You must already dare you will become then truly

meine Frau, und dann haben die andern dir nichts zu
my wife and then have the others you nothing to

befehlen."
order

"Aber meine Mutter wird weinen."
But my mother will cry

"Wir kommen ja wieder," sagte Reinhard heftig;
We come yes back said Reinhard strongly
(of course)

"sag es nur gerade heraus, willst du mit mir reisen?
say it just straight out want you with me travel

Sonst geh' ich allein, und dann komme ich nimmer
Otherwise go I alone and then come I never

wieder."
again

Der Kleinen kam das Weinen nahe. "Mach nur nicht
The little one came the crying close Make just not

so böse Augen," sagte sie; "ich will ja mit nach
such angry eyes said she I want indeed along to

Indien."
India

Reinhard faßte sie mit ausgelassener Freude bei
Reinhard grabbed her with let-out happiness at
(lively)

beiden Händen und zog sie hinaus auf die Wiese.
both hands and pulled her out on the meadow

"Nach Indien, nach Indien!" sang er und schwenkte
To India to India sang he and turned

sich mit ihr im Kreise, daß ihr das rote
himself with her in the circle (so) that her the red

13

Tüchelchen vom Halse flog. Dann aber ließ er sie
little cloth from the neck flew Then however let he her

plötzlich los und sagte ernst:
suddenly loose and said seriously

"Es wird doch nichts daraus werden; du hast keine
It will however nothing there from become you have no

Courage."
courage

"Elisabeth! Reinhard!" rief es jetzt von der
Elisabeth Reinhard called it now from the

Gartenpforte. "Hier! Hier!" antworteten die Kinder und
garden gate Here Here answered the children and

sprangen Hand in Hand nach Hause.
ran hand in hand to house
home

Im Walde

Im Walde
In the Forest

So lebten die Kinder zusammen; sie war ihm oft zu
Thus lived the children together she was him often too

still, er war ihr oft zu heftig, aber sie ließen
quiet he was her often too lively but they let
(left)

deshalb nicht von einander; fast alle Freistunden
despite that not from each other almost all free hours

teilten sie: winters in den beschränkten Zimmern ihrer
shared they in winter in the cramped rooms of their

Mütter, sommers in Busch und Feld.
mothers in summer in bush and field

Als Elisabeth einmal in Reinhards Gegenwart von dem
As Elisabeth once in Reinhards presence by the

Schullehrer gescholten wurde, stieß er seine Tafel
schoolteacher scolded became banged he his tablet
(abacus)

zornig auf den Tisch, um den Eifer des Mannes auf
angrily on the table for the zeal of the man on

sich zu lenken. Es wurde nicht bemerkt.
himself to direct It became not noticed

15

Aber Reinhard verlor alle Aufmerksamkeit an den
But Reinhard lost all attention on the

geographischen Vorträgen; statt dessen verfaßte er ein
geographical lectures instead of that created he a

langes Gedicht; darin verglich er sich selbst mit
long poem there-in compared he himself self with

einem jungen Adler, den Schulmeister mit einer grauen
a young eagle the schoolteacher with a gray

Krähe, Elisabeth war die weiße Taube; der Adler
crow Elisabeth was the white dove the eagle

gelobte an der grauen Krähe Rache zu nehmen, sobald
promised on the gray crow revenge to take as soon

ihm die Flügel gewachsen sein würden.
him the wings grown been would

Dem jungen Dichter standen die Tränen in den Augen;
The young poet stood the tears in the eyes

er kam sich sehr erhaben vor. Als er nach Hause
he came himself very lofty before As he to house

gekommen war, wußte er sich einen kleinen
came was knew he himself a little

Pergamentband mit vielen weißen Blättern zu
parchment band with many white leaves to
(pages)

verschaffen; auf die ersten Seiten schrieb er mit
acquire on the first sides wrote he with

sorgsamer Hand sein erstes Gedicht.
careful hand his first poem

16

Bald darauf kam er in eine andere Schule; hier schloß
Soon there-on came he in an other school here locked
(made)

er manche neue Kameradschaft mit Knaben seines
he many (a) new comradeship with boys of his
(friendship)

Alters, aber sein Verkehr mit Elisabeth wurde
age but his traffic with Elisabeth became
(relationship)

dadurch nicht gestört. Von den Märchen, welche er
there-through not disturbed Of the fairytales which he

ihr sonst erzählt und wieder erzählt hatte,
her usually told and again told had

fing er jetzt an, die, welche ihr am besten gefallen
caught he now on those which her to the best pleased
started he now

hatten, aufzuschreiben; dabei
had on-to-write there-by
(to write down)

wandelte ihn oft die Lust etwas von seinen
walked him often the lust something from his
an,
on
it often came over him

eigenen Gedanken hineinzudichten; aber, er wußte nicht
own thoughts to weave in however he knew not

weshalb, er konnte immer nicht dazu gelangen.
how he could never not to it succeed

So schrieb er sie genau auf, wie er sie selber
So wrote he them exactly on as he them self
(down)

gehört hatte. Dann gab er die Blätter an Elisabeth,
heard had Then gave he the pages to Elisabeth

17

die sie in einem Schubfach ihrer Schatulle sorgfältig
who them in a drawer of her casket carefully

aufbewahrte; und es gewährte ihm eine anmutige
guarded and it granted him an encouraging

Befriedigung, wenn er sie mitunter abends diese
satisfaction when he her during (the) evening these

Geschichtchen in seiner Gegenwart aus den von ihm
little stories in his presence from the by him

geschriebenen Heften ihrer Mutter vorlesen hörte.
written notebooks to her mother read to heard

Sieben Jahre waren vorüber. Reinhard sollte zu seiner
Seven years were past Reinhard must for his

weitern Ausbildung die Stadt verlassen. Elisabeth konnte
further education the city leave Elisabeth could

sich nicht in den Gedanken finden, daß es nun eine
herself not in the thought find that it now a
(there)

Zeit ganz ohne Reinhard geben werde. Es freute sie,
time all without Reinhard give would It pleased her

als er ihr eines Tages sagte, er werde, wie sonst,
when he her one day said he would as usual

Märchen für sie aufschreiben; er wolle sie ihr mit
fairytales for her write down he wanted them her with

den Briefen an seine Mutter schicken; sie müsse ihm
the letters to his mother send she must him

dann wieder schreiben, wie sie ihr gefallen hätten.
then again write how they her pleased had

18

Die	Abreise	rückte	heran;	vorher	aber	kam	noch
The	parting	drew	close	before	however	came	still

mancher	Reim	in	den	Pergamentband.	Das	allein	war
often	rhyme	in	the	parchment band	That	alone	was

für	Elisabeth	ein	Geheimnis,	obgleich	sie	die
for	Elisabeth	a	secret	although	she	the

Veranlassung	zu	dem	ganzen	Buche	und	zu	den
instigation	to	the	whole	book	and	to	the

meisten	Liedern	war,	welche	nach	und	nach	fast	die
most	songs (verses)	was	which	after	and on and on	after	almost	~~the~~

Hälfte	der	weißen	Blätter	gefüllt	hatten.
half	of the	white	leaves	filled	had

Es	war	im	Juni;	Reinhard	sollte	am	andern	Tage
It	was	in	June	Reinhard	must	on the	other (next)	day

reisen.	Nun	wollte	man	noch	einmal	einen	festlichen
travel	Now	wanted	one (they)	still	once	a	festive

Tag	zusammen	begehen.	Dazu	wurde	eine	Landpartie
day	together	go on	There-to	was	an	outing

nach	einer	der	nahe	gelegenen	Holzungen	in	größerer
to	one	of the	close	situated	woodlands	in	larger

Gesellschaft	veranstaltet.
company	organized

19

Der	stundenlange	Weg	bis	an	den	Saum	des	Waldes
The	hours-long	road	until	on	the	edge	of the	forest

wurde	zu	Wagen	zurückgelegt;	dann	nahm	man	die
became	on	cart	back-laid (taken)	then	took	they	the

Proviantkörbe	herunter	und	marschierte	weiter.	Ein
food-basket	down	and	walked	further	A

Tannengehölz	mußte	zuerst	durchwandert	werden;	es	war
fir woodland	must	first	through walked	become	it	was

kühl	und	dämmerig	und	der	Boden	überall	mit	feinen
cool	and	a little dark	and	the	ground	everywhere	with	fine

Nadeln	bestreut.
needles	strewn

Nach	halbstündigem	Wandern	kam	man	aus	dem
After	(an) half hour	walking	came	they	out (of)	the

Tannendunkel	in	eine	frische	Buchenwaldung;	hier	war
fir darkness	in(to)	a	fresh	beech wood	here	was

alles	licht	und	grün;	mitunter	brach	ein	Sonnenstrahl
everything	light	and	green	meanwhile	broke	a	sunbeam

durch	die	blätterreichen	Zweige;	ein	Eichkätzchen	sprang
through	the	leaf-rich	branches	a	oak-little cat (squirrel)	jumped

über	ihren	Köpfen	von	Ast	zu	Ast.
over	their	heads	from	branch	to	branch

20

Auf einem Platze, über welchem uralte Buchen mit
On one place over which ancient beeches with

ihren Kronen zu einem durchsichtigen Laubgewölbe
their crowns to a transparent foliage vault
(foliage roof)

zusammenwuchsen, machte die Gesellschaft Halt.
together grew made the company halt

Elisabeths Mutter öffnete einen der Körbe; ein alter
Elisabeth's mother opened one of the baskets an old

Herr warf sich zum Proviantmeister auf.
gentleman threw himself as the food master on
posed as purser

"Alle um mich herum, ihr jungen Vögel!" rief er,
All around me around you young birds called he

"und merket genau, was ich euch zu sagen habe. Zum
and note exactly what I you to say have To the

Frühstück erhält jetzt ein jeder von euch zwei
breakfast receives now one each of you two

trockene Wecken; die Butter ist zu Hause
dry long white breads the butter is at home

geblieben; die Zukost muß sich ein jeder selber
remained the to-food must themselves one each self
(garnish)

suchen. Es stehen genug Erdbeeren im Walde, das
search It stand enough strawberries in the forest that
There are

heißt, für den, der sie zu finden weiß. Wer
means for the one who them to find knows Who

ungeschickt ist, muß sein Brot trocken essen; so geht
unable is must their bread dry eat so goes

21

es überall im Leben. Habt ihr meine Rede
it everywhere in the life Have you my speech

begriffen?"
understood

"Ja wohl!" riefen die Jungen.
Yes well called (out) the young (ones)
(indeed)

"Ja, seht," sagte der Alte, "sie ist aber noch
Yes see said the old (one) she is however yet
(the speech)

nicht zu Ende. Wir Alten haben uns im Leben
not to end We old (ones) have us in the life

schon genug umhergetrieben; darum bleiben wir jetzt
already enough around driven therefore stay we now
(busied)

zu Haus, das heißt, hier unter diesen breiten Bäumen,
at home that means here under these wide trees

und schälen die Kartoffeln und machen Feuer und
and peel the potatoes and make fire and

rüsten die Tafel, und wenn die Uhr zwölf ist, so
set the table and when the hour twelve is so

sollen auch die Eier gekocht werden."
must also the eggs boiled become

"Dafür seid ihr uns von euren Erdbeeren die Hälfte
There-for are you us from your strawberries the half
(For that)

schuldig, damit wir auch einen Nachtisch servieren
guilty there-with we also a after-platter serve
(owing)

22

können. Und nun geht nach Ost und West und seid
can   And now go to   east and west and be

ehrlich."
honest

Die Jungen machten allerlei schelmische Gesichter.
The young ones made all kinds of naughty faces

"Halt!" rief der alte Herr noch einmal. "Das
Stop called out the old gentleman still once That

brauche ich euch wohl nicht zu sagen, wer keine
need I you well not to say who none
(also)

findet, braucht auch keine abzuliefern; aber das schreibt
finds needs also none to deliver but that write

euch wohl hinter eure feinen Ohren, von uns Alten
you well behind your fine ears from us old ones

bekommt er auch nichts. Und nun habt ihr für diesen
gets he also nothing And now have you for this

Tag gute Lehren genug; wenn ihr nun noch Erdbeeren
day good learning enough when you now still strawberries

dazu habt, so werdet ihr für heute schon
there-to have so will you for today already
(on top of that)

durchs Leben kommen."
through the life come

Die Jungen waren derselben Meinung und begannen
The young ones were of the same opinion and began

sich paarweise auf die Fahrt zu machen.
themselves in pairs on the journey to make
(go)

"Komm, Elisabeth," sagte Reinhard, "ich weiß einen
Come Elisabeth said Reinhard I know a

Erdbeerenschlag; du sollst kein trockenes Brot essen."
strawberry patch you must not dry bread eat

Elisabeth knüpfte die grünen Bänder ihres Strohhuts
Elisabeth knotted the green bands of her straw hat

zusammen und hing ihn über den Arm. "So komm,"
together and hung it over the arm So come

sagte sie, "der Korb ist fertig."
said she the basket is ready

Dann gingen sie in den Wald hinein, tiefer und tiefer;
Then went they in the forest inside deeper and deeper

durch feuchte Baumschatten, wo alles still war,
through moist tree shades where everything quiet was

nur unsichtbar über ihnen in den Lüften das Geschrei
only invisible above them in the air the cry

der Falken; dann wieder durch dichtes Gestrüpp, so
of the falcon then again through close brushwood so

dicht, daß Reinhard vorangehen mußte, um einen Pfad
close that Reinhard in front go must for a path

24

zu machen, hier einen Zweig zu knicken, dort eine
to make hier a branch to snap there a

Ranke beiseite zu biegen. Bald aber hörte er hinter
shoot to the side to bend Soon however heard he behind

sich Elisabeth seinen Namen rufen. Er wandte sich
himself Elisabeth his name call He turned himself

um.
around

"Reinhard!" rief sie, "warte doch, Reinhard!"
Reinhard called she (out) wait indeed Reinhard
                             wait please

Er konnte sie nicht gewahr werden; endlich sah er sie
He could her not aware of become finally saw he her

in einiger Entfernung mit den Sträuchern kämpfen; ihr
in some distance with the bushes battle her
                                      (struggle)

feines Köpfchen schwamm nur kaum über den Spitzen
fine little head swam only hardly over the tops

der Farnkräuter. Nun ging er noch einmal zurück und
of the ferns Now went he yet one time back and

führte sie durch das Wirrnis der Kräuter und Stauden
led her through the tangle of the herbs and perennials
                                      (plants)

auf einen freien Platz hinaus, wo blaue Falter
on a free place to-out where blue butterflies
                (clear)

zwischen den einsamen Waldblumen flatterten.
between the lonely forest flowers fluttered

25

Reinhard	strich	ihr	die	feuchten	Haare	aus	dem
Reinhard	brushed	her	the	wet	hair	from	the

erhitzten	Gesichtchen;	dann	wollte	er	ihr	den	Strohhut
heated (flushed)	little face	then	wanted	he	her	the	straw hat

aufsetzen,	und	sie	wollte	es	nicht	leiden;	aber	dann
put on	and	she	wanted	it	not	suffer (tolerate)	but	then

bat	er	sie,	und	nun	ließ	sie	es	doch	geschehen.
bade	he	her	and	now	let	she	it	still	happen

"Wo	bleiben	denn	aber	deine	Erdbeeren?"	fragte	sie
Where	stay	then	however	your	strawberries	asked	she
What's keeping							

endlich,	indem	sie	stehen	blieb	und	einen	tiefen
finally	while	she	stand	remained	and	a	deep

Atemzug	tat.
breath draw	did
breath took	

"Hier	haben	sie	gestanden,"	sagte	er,	"aber	die	Kröten
Here	have	they	stood	said	he	but	the	toads

sind	uns	zuvorgekommen	oder	die	Marder	oder
are	us	before come	or	the	marter	or
		were first				

vielleicht	die	Elfen."
maybe	the	elves

"Ja," sagte Elisabeth, "die Blätter stehen noch da; aber
Yes said Elisabeth the leaves stand still there but

sprich hier nicht von Elfen. Komm nur, ich bin noch
speak here not from Elves Come only I am still

gar nicht müde; wir wollen weiter suchen."
at all not tired we want further search

Vor ihnen war ein kleiner Bach, jenseits
Before them was a small stream on the other side of it

wieder der Wald. Reinhard hob Elisabeth auf seine
again the forest Reinhard lifted Elisabeth on his

Arme und trug sie hinüber. Nach einer Weile traten
arms and carried her over After a while stepped

sie aus dem schattigen Laube wieder in eine weite
they from the shaded foliage again in a wide

Lichtung hinaus.
clearing out

"Hier müssen Erdbeeren sein," sagte das Mädchen, "es
Here must strawberries be said the girl it

duftet so süß."
smells so sweet

27

Sie	gingen	suchend	durch	den	sonnigen	Raum;	aber
They	went	searching	through	the	sunny	space	but

sie	fanden	keine.	"Nein,"	sagte	Reinhard,	"es	ist	nur
they	found	none	No	said	Reinhard	it	is	only

der	Duft	des	Heidekrautes."
the	fragrance	of the	heath herbs

Himbeerbüsche	und	Hülsendorn	standen	überall
Raspberry bushes	and	holly thorn	stood	everywhere

durcheinander,	ein	starker	Geruch	von	Heidekräutern,
through each other (mixed)	a	strong	smell	of	heath herbs

welche	abwechselnd	mit	kurzem	Grase	die	freien	Stellen
which	exchanging (alternated)	with	short	grass	the	free	spots

des	Bodens	bedeckten,	erfüllte	die	Luft.
of the	bottom (ground)	covered	filled	the	air

"Hier	ist	es	einsam,"	sagte	Elisabeth;	"wo	mögen	die
Here	is	it	lonely	said	Elisabeth	where	may	the

andern	sein?"
others	be

An	den	Rückweg	hatte	Reinhard	nicht	gedacht.
On (Of)	the	way back	had	Reinhard	not	thought

"Warte nur: woher kommt der Wind?" sagte er und
Wait just from where comes the wind said he and

hob seine Hand in die Höhe. Aber es kam kein
raised his hand in the height But it came no
up there was

Wind.
wind

"Still," sagte Elisabeth, "mich dünkt, ich hörte sie
Quiet said Elisabeth (to) me (it) seems I heard them

sprechen. Rufe einmal dahinunter."
speak Call one time there to down
(over there)

Reinhard rief durch die hohle Hand. "Kommt hierher!"
Reinhard called through the hollow hand Come here

"Hierher!" rief es zurück.
Here called it back

"Sie antworteten!" sagte Elisabeth und klatschte in die
They answer said Elisabeth and clapped in the

Hände.
hands

"Nein, es war nichts, es war nur der Widerhall."
No it was nothing it was just the echo

Elisabeth faßte Reinhards Hand. "Mir graut!" sagte
Elisabeth gripped Reinhards hand To me (it) dreads said
I'm scared

sie.
she

"Nein," sagte Reinhard, "das muß es nicht. Hier ist es
No said Reinhard that must it not Here is it

prächtig. Setz dich dort in den Schatten zwischen die
wonderful Set yourself there in the shade between the

Kräuter. Laß uns eine Weile ausruhen; wir finden die
herbs Let us a while rest we find the

andern schon."
others already
(later)

Elisabeth setzte sich unter eine überhängende Buche
Elisabeth set herself under an overhanging beech

und lauschte aufmerksam nach allen Seiten; Reinhard
and heard attentively to all sides Reinhard

saß einige Schritte davon auf einem Baumstumpf und
sat some steps there-from on a tree stump and

sah schweigend nach ihr hinüber.
looked in silence at her over

Die Sonne stand gerade über ihnen; es war
The sun stood straight over them it was

glühende Mittagshitze; kleine goldglänzende, stahlblaue
glowing midday heat small gold shimmering steel blue
searing afternoon heat

30

Fliegen standen flügelschwingend in der Luft; rings
flies stood wings flailing in the air in a circle

um sie her ein feines Schwirren und Summen, und
around them ~~to~~ a fine buzzing and zooming and

manchmal hörte man tief im Walde das Hämmern
often heard one deep in the forest the hammering
(they)

der Spechte und das Kreischen der andern
of the woodpeckers and the crying of the other

Waldvögel.
forest birds

"Horch," sagte Elisabeth, "es läutet."
Hear said Elisabeth it sounds

"Wo?" fragte Reinhard.
Where asked Reinhard

"Hinter uns. Hörst du? Es ist Mittag."
Behind us hear you It is midday

"Dann liegt hinter uns die Stadt, und wenn wir in
Then lies behind us the town and when we in

dieser Richtung gerade durchgehen, so müssen wir die
this direction straight go on then must we the

andern treffen."
others meet

So traten sie ihren Rückweg das Erdbeerensuchen an;
So stepped they their way back the strawberry searching on

So started they their return journey

hatten sie aufgegeben, denn Elisabeth war müde
had they given up since Elisabeth was (had) tired

geworden. Endlich klang zwischen den Bäumen hindurch
become Finally sounded between the trees through

das Lachen der Gesellschaft; dann sahen sie auch ein
the laughing of the company then saw they also a

weißes Tuch am Boden schimmern, das war die Tafel,
white cloth on the ground glint that was the table

und darauf standen Erdbeeren in Hülle und Fülle.
and there upon stood strawberries in shell and abundance

Der alte Herr hatte eine Serviette im Knopfloch
The old gentleman had a napkin in the button hole

und hielt den Jungen die Fortsetzung seiner
and held the young ones the continuation of his

moralischen Reden, während er eifrig an einem
moralistic speech while he zealously on a

Braten herumtranchierte.
roast meat carved around

"Da sind die Nachzügler," riefen die Jungen, als sie
There are the afterpullers called the young ones as they
(latecomers)

Reinhard und Elisabeth durch die Bäume kommen
Reinhard and Elisabeth through the trees come

sahen.
saw

"Hierher!" rief der alte Herr, "Tücher ausgeleert,
Here-to called the old gentleman cloths emptied

Hüte umgekehrt! Nun zeigt her, was ihr gefunden
hats turned over Now show here what you found

habt."
have

"Hunger und Durst!" sagte Reinhard.
Hunger and thirst said Reinhard

"Wenn, das alles ist," erwiderte der Alte und hob
When that everything is responded the old one and lifted

ihnen die volle Schüssel entgegen, "so müßt ihr es
them the full dish against so must you it
(away from)

auch behalten. Ihr kennt die Abrede; hier werden keine
also keep You know the deal here become no

Müßiggänger gefüttert."
loafers fed

33

Endlich	ließ	er	sich	aber	doch	erbitten,	und	nun
Finally	let	he	himself	however	still	convince	and	now

wurde	Tafel	gehalten;	dazu	schlug	die	Drossel	aus
became	table	held	there-to	struck (sang)	the	thrush	from

den	Wacholderbüschen.
the	juniper bushes

So	ging	der	Tag	hin.	Reinhard	hatte	aber	doch
So	went	the	day	away	Reinhard	had	however	yet

etwas	gefunden;	waren	es	keine	Erdbeeren,	so	war
something	found	were	it	no	strawbarries	so	was

es	doch	auch	im	Walde	gewachsen.	Als	er
it	however	also	in the	forest	grown	When	he

nach	Hause	gekommen	war,	schrieb	er	in	seinen	alten
to	house home	come	was (had)	wrote	he	in	his	old

Pergamentband:
parchment band (vellum)

Hier	an	der	Bergeshalde
Here	by	the	mountain slope

Verstummet	ganz	der	Wind;
Silences	totally	the	wind

Die	Zweige	hängen	nieder,
The	branches	hang	down

34

Darunter sitzt das Kind
There under sits the child

Sie sitzt im Thymiane,
She sits in the thyme

Sie sitzt in lauter Duft;
She sits in pure fragrance

Die blauen Fliegen summen
The blue flies buzz

Und blitzen durch die Luft.
And flash through the air

Es steht der Wald so schweigend,
It stands the forest so in silence
The forest stands

Sie schaut so klug darein;
She peers so wise there-in

Um ihre braunen Locken
Around her brown curls

Hinfließt der Sonnenschein.
Goes the sunshine

Der Kuckuck lacht von ferne,
The cuckoo laughs from afar

Es geht mir durch den Sinn:
It goes me through the mind

Sie hat die goldnen Augen
She has the golden eyes

Der Waldeskönigin.
Of the forest queen

So war sie nicht allein sein Schützling, sie war ihm
Thus was she not just his protegee she was to him

auch der Ausdruck für alles Liebliche und Wunderbare
also the expression for all (the) dear and wonderful

seines aufgehenden Lebens.
of his up-going life
(dawning)

Da Stand Das Kind Am Wege

Da	Stand	Das	Kind	Am	Wege
There	stood	the	child	by the	road

Weihnachtsabend	kam	heran.	Es	war	noch	nachmittags,
Christmas eve	came	up	It	was	still	afternoon

als	Reinhard	mit	andern	Studenten	im	Ratskeller
when	Reinhard	with	other	students	in the	Council cellar

(Rathauskeller)	am	alten	Eichentisch	zusammensaß.	Die
Council house cellar (City hall, Pub)	at the	old	oak table	together sat	The

Lampen	an	den	Wänden	waren	angezündet,	denn	hier
lamps	at	the	walls	were	lit	since	here

unten	dämmerte	es	schon;	aber	die	Gäste	waren
down	was getting dark	it	already	but	the	guests	were

sparsam	versammelt,	die	Kellner	lehnten	müßig	an	den
sparingly	gathered	the	waiters	leaned	idly	on	the

Mauerpfeilern.
wall-supports

In	einem	Winkel	des	Gewölbes	saßen	ein	Geigenspieler
In	a	corner	of the	vault	sat	a	violin player

und	ein	Zithermädchen	mit	feinen	zigeunerhaften	Zügen;
and	a	zither girl	with	fine	gipsy like	traits

sie hatten ihre Instrumente auf dem Schoß liegen und
they had their instruments on the lap lay and

schienen teilnahmslos vor sich hinzusehen.
seemed without taking part before themselves to see

Am Studententische knallte ein Champagnerpfropfen.
At the student table banged a champagne cork

"Trinke, mein böhmisch Liebchen!" rief ein junger
Drink my bohemian dear called out a young

Mann von junkerhaftem Äußern, indem er ein volles
man from noble expression while he a full
(with)

Glas zu dem Mädchen hinüberreichte.
glass to the girl reached over

"Ich mag nicht," sagte sie, ohne ihre Stellung zu
I may not said she without her position to
I don't like it

verändern.
change

"So singe!" rief der Junker und warf ihr eine
Then sing called out the young noble and threw her a

Silbermünze in den Schoß. Das Mädchen strich sich
silver coin in the lap The girl brushed herself

langsam mit den Fingern durch ihr schwarzes Haar,
slowly with the fingers through her black hair

während der Geigenspieler ihr ins Ohr flüsterte; aber
while the violin player her in the ear whispered but

38

sie warf den Kopf zurück und stützte das Kinn auf
she threw the head back and supported the chin on
(leaned)

ihre Zither.
her zither

"Für den spiel' ich nicht," sagte sie.
For that play I not said she

Reinhard sprang mit dem Glase in der Hand auf und
Reinhard jumped with the glass in the hand up and

stellte sich vor sie.
put himself before her

"Was willst du?" fragte sie trotzig.
What want you asked she defiant
What do you want

"Deine Augen sehen."
Your eyes see

"Was geh'n dich meine Augen
What go you my eyes
an?"
on
What business are my eyes to you

Reinhard sah funkelnd auf sie nieder.
Reinhard looked scintillating on her down

39

"Ich weiß wohl, sie sind falsch!"
I know well they are false

Sie legte ihre Wange in die flache Hand und
She put her cheek in the flat hand and

sah ihn lauernd an. Reinhard hob sein Glas an den
looked him spying at Reinhard raised his glass to the
looked at him slit eyed

Mund.
mouth

"Auf deine schönen sündhaften Augen!" sagte er und
On your beautiful sinful eyes said he and
(To)

trank.
drank

Sie lachte und warf den Kopf herum.
She laughed and threw the

"Gib!" sagte sie, und indem sie ihre schwarzen Augen
Give said she and while she her black eyes

in die seinen heftete, trank sie langsam den Rest.
in the his pinned drank she slowly the rest

Dann griff sie einen Dreiklang und sang mit tiefer
Then grabbed she a triad and sang with deep

leidenschaftlicher Stimme:
passionate voice

40

Heute, nur heute Bin ich so schön, Morgen, ach
Today only today am I so beautiful Tomorrow ah

morgen Muß alles vergeh'n! Nur diese Stunde Bist du
tomorrow Must all perish Only this hour Are you

noch mein; Sterben, ach sterben Soll ich allein!
still mine Die ah die will I alone

Während der Geigenspieler in raschem Tempo das
While the violin player in quick tempo the

Nachspiel einsetzte, gesellte sich ein neuer Ankömmling
after play set in joined himself a new arrival

zu der Gruppe.
to the group

"Ich wollte dich abholen, Reinhard," sagte er. "Du
I wanted you fetch Reinhard said he You

warst schon fort; aber das Christkind war bei dir
were already gone but the Christ child was by you

eingekehrt."
moved in

"Das Christkind?" sagte Reinhard, "das kommt nicht
The Christ child said Reinhard that comes not

mehr zu mir."
(any)more to me

41

"Ei was! Dein ganzes Zimmer roch nach Tannenbaum
Eh what Your whole room smelled like christmas tree

und braunen Kuchen."
and brown cake

Reinhard setzte das Glas aus seiner Hand und griff
Reinhard set the glass from his hand and grabbed

nach seiner Mütze.
after his hat

"Was willst du?" fragte das Mädchen.
What want you asked the girl

"Ich komme schon wieder."
I come indeed again

Sie runzelte die Stirn. "Bleib!" rief sie leise und
She frowned the forehead Stay called she slow and

sah ihn vertraulich an.
looked him confidentially at
looked at him with a confidential expression

Reinhard zögerte. "Ich kann nicht," sagte er.
Reinhard hesitated I can not said he

Sie	stieß	ihn	lachend	mit	der	Fußspitze.	"Geh!"	sagte
She	bumped	him	laughing	with	the	foot point	Go	said

sie,	"du	taugst	nichts;	ihr	taugt	alle	mit	einander
she	you	are worthy	not	you	are worthy	all	with	each other

nichts."	Und	während	sie	sich	abwandte,	stieg
nothing	And	while	she	herself	turned away	mounted

Reinhard	langsam	die	Kellertreppe	hinauf.
Reinhard	slowly	the	Cellar stairs	to-up

Draußen	auf	der	Straße	war	es	tiefe	Dämmerung;	er
Outside	on	the	street	was	it	deep	dusk	he

fühlte	die	frische	Winterluft	an	seiner	heißen	Stirn.
felt	the	fresh	winter air	to	his	hot	forehead

Hier	und	da	fiel	der	helle	Schein	eines	brennenden
Here	and	there	fell	the	bright	shine	of a	burning (lit)

Tannenbaums	aus	den	Fenstern,	dann	und	wann	hörte
christmas tree	from	the	windows	then	and	when	heard
						now and then	

man	von	drinnen	das	Geräusch	von	kleinen	Pfeifen	und
one	from	inside	the	sound	of	small	flutes	and

Blechtrompeten	und	dazwischen	jubelnde	Kinderstimmen.
trumpets	and	in between	rejoicing	children's voices

Scharen	von	Bettelkindern	gingen	von	Haus	zu	Haus
Flocks	of	beggar children	went	from	house	to	house

oder	stiegen	auf	die	Treppengeländer	und	suchten
or	climbed	up	the	stair platforms	and	searched

43

durch	die	Fenster	einen	Blick	in	die	versagte
through	the	windows	a	glance	in	the	denied

Herrlichkeit	zu	gewinnen.	Mitunter	wurde	auch	eine
greatness	to	win	Middle-under	became	also	a
			(From time to time)			

Tür	plötzlich	aufgerissen,	und	scheltende	Stimmen
door	suddenly	up-torn	and	scolding	voices
		(quickly opened)			

trieben	einen	ganzen	Schwarm	solcher	kleinen	Gäste
drove	a	whole	swarm	of such	small	guests

aus	dem	hellen	Hause	auf	die	dunkle	Gasse	hinaus;
from	the	bright	house	on(to)	the	dark	alley	-to-out-

anderswo	wurde	auf	dem	Hausflur	ein	altes
elsewhere	became	on	the	house floor	an	old
				(second floor with living room)		

Weihnachtslied	gesungen;	es	waren	klare
Christmas song	sung	it	were	clear
		(there)		

Mädchenstimmen	darunter.
girls voices	there-under
	(between them)

Reinhard	hörte	sie	nicht,	er	ging	rasch	an	allem
Reinhard	heard	them	not	he	went	quick	to	all

vorüber,	aus	einer	Straße	in	die	andere.	Als	er	an
past	from	one	street	in(to)	the	other	As	he	to

seine	Wohnung	gekommen,	war	es	fast	völlig	dunkel
his	apartment	come (had)	was	it	almost	totally	dark

geworden;	er	stolperte	die	Treppe	hinauf	und	trat
become	he	stumbled	the	stairs	up	and	stepped

in	seine	Stube.
in(to)	his	room

Ein	süßer	Duft	schlug	ihm	entgegen;		das
A	sweet	smell	struck	him	against		that
					met him		

heimelte	ihn	an,	das	roch	wie	zu	Haus	der	Mutter
homelied	him	on	it	smelled	as	at	home	the	mother's
made him feel at home									

Weihnachtsstube.	Mit	zitternder	Hand	zündete	er	sein
Christmas room	With	trembling	hand	lit	he	his

Licht	an;	da	lag	ein	mächtiges	Paket	auf	dem	Tisch,
light	on	there	lay	a	great	package	on	the	table

und	als	er	es	öffnete,	fielen	die	wohlbekannten
and	when	he	it	opened	fell	the	well known

braunen	Festkuchen	heraus;	auf	einigen	waren	die
brown	party-cakes	out	on	some	were	the

Anfangsbuchstaben	seines	Namens	in	Zucker	ausgestreut;
beginning-letters	of his	name	in	sugar	strewn
(initials)					

das	konnte	niemand	anders	als	Elisabeth	getan	haben.
that	could	nobody	else	as	Elisabeth	done	have

Dann	kam	ein	Päckchen	mit	feiner	gestickter	Wäsche
Then	came	a	little package	with	fine	embroidered	wash
							(clothing)

zum	Vorschein,	Tücher	und	Manschetten,	zuletzt	Briefe
to the	appearance	cloths	and	cuffs	at last	letters
	to light					

von	der	Mutter	und	Elisabeth.	Reinhard	öffnete	zuerst
from	the	mother	and	Elisabeth	Reinhard	opened	first

den	letzteren;	Elisabeth	schrieb:
the	last	Elisabeth	wrote

Die schönen Zuckerbuchstaben können Dir wohl erzählen,
The beautiful sugar-letters can you well relate

wer bei den Kuchen mitgeholfen hat; dieselbe Person
who by the cakes helped along has the same person

hat die Manschetten für Dich gestickt. Bei uns wird
has the cuffs for you embroidered By us will

es nun am Weihnachtsabend sehr still werden; meine
it now on the Christmas evening very quiet become my

Mutter stellt immer schon um halb zehn ihr
mother sets always already at half ten her

Spinnrad in die Ecke; es ist gar so einsam diesen
Spinning wheel in the corner it is indeed so lonely this

Winter, wo Du nicht hier bist.
winter where you not here are

Nun ist auch vorigen Sonntag der Hänfling gestorben,
Now is also last Sunday the linnet bird died

den Du mir geschenkt hattest; ich habe sehr
that you me send had I have very much

geweint, aber ich hab' ihn doch immer gut gewartet.
cried but I have him however always well waited (on)
(served)

Der sang sonst immer nachmittags, wenn die Sonne
It sang usually always in the afternoons when the sun

auf sein Bauer schien; Du weißt, die Mutter hing so
on his birdcage shone You know the mother hung so
(archaic)

oft ein Tuch über, um ihn zu geschweigen, wenn er
often a cloth over (it) for him to silence when he

so recht aus Kräften sang.
so right from strength sang

Da ist es nun noch stiller in der Kammer, nur
Then is it now even more quiete in the room only

daß Dein alter Freund Erich uns jetzt mitunter
that your old friend Eric us now from time to time

besucht. Du sagtest uns einmal, er sähe seinem
visits You told us once he sees his
(looks)

braunen Überrock ähnlich. Daran muß ich nun immer
brown overcoat like There-on must I now always

denken, wenn er zur Tür hereinkommt, und es ist
think when he to the door in comes and it is

gar zu komisch; sag es aber nicht zur Mutter, sie
all too comical say it however not to the mother she

wird dann leicht verdrießlich.
becomes then easily sad

Rat, was ich Deiner Mutter zu Weihnachten schenke!
Guess what I your mother to Christmas night give

Du rätst es nicht? Mich selber! Der Erich
You guess it not My self The Eric

47

zeichnet mich in schwarzer   ich   habe   ihm
draws me in black   I   have   him
Kreide;
chalk
bores me to death

dreimal sitzen müssen, jedesmal eine ganze Stunde.
three times sit must each time a whole hour
(receive)

Es war mir recht zuwider, daß der fremde Mensch
It was me really unpleasant that the strange human
(man)

mein Gesicht so auswendig lernte. Ich wollte auch
my face thus by heart learns I wanted also

nicht, aber die Mutter redete mir zu; sie sagte, es
not but the mother talks me to she said it

würde der guten Frau Werner eine gar große Freude
will the good mrs. Werner a very great joy
(Eric's mother)

machen.
make
(do)

Aber Du hältst nicht Wort, Reinhard. Du hast keine
But you keep not word Reinhard You have no

Märchen geschickt. Ich habe Dich oft bei Deiner
fairy tales send I have you often by your

Mutter verklagt; sie sagt dann immer, Du habest
mother complained (about) she says then always You have

jetzt mehr zu tun, als solche Kindereien. Ich glaub' es
now more to do as such childishnesses I believe it

aber nicht; es ist wohl anders."
however not it is well different

Nun	las	Reinhard	auch	den	Brief	seiner	Mutter,	und
Now	read	Reinhard	also	the	letter	of his	mother	and

als	er	beide	Briefe	gelesen	und	langsam	wieder
when	he	both	letters	read	and	slowly	again

zusammengefaltet	und	weggelegt	hatte,	überfiel	ihn	ein
together folded	and	put away	had	fell over	him	a

unerbittliches	Heimweh.	Er	ging	eine	Zeitlang	in
inexorable	homesickness	He	went	a	time long	in

seinem	Zimmer	auf	und	nieder:	er	sprach	leise	und
his	room	up	and	down	he	spoke	slow	and

dann	halbverständlich	zu	sich	selbst:
then	half understandible	to	himself	~~self~~

Er	wäre	fast	verirret
He	was (had)	almost	gone astray

Und	wußte	nicht	hinaus;
And	knew	not	to-out (the way out)

Da	stand	das	Kind	am	Wege
There	stood	the	child	on the	road

Und	winkte	ihm	nach	Haus.
And	waved (beckoned)	him	to	house home

Dann	trat	er	an	sein	Pult,	nahm	einiges	Geld
Then	stepped	he	to	his	desk	took	some	money

heraus	und	ging	wieder	auf	die	Straße	hinab.	Hier
out	and	went	again	on	the	street	down	Here

war	es	mittlerweile	stiller	geworden;	die
was	it	meanwhile	more quiet	become	the

Weihnachtsbäume	waren	ausgebrannt,	die	Umzüge
christmas trees	were	burned out (extinguished)	the	movings around

der	Kinder	hatten	aufgehört.	Der	Wind	fegte	durch
of the	children	had	stopped	The	wind	swept	through

die	einsamen	Straßen;	Alte	und	Junge	saßen	in
the	lonely	streets	old ones	and	young ones	sat	in

ihren	Häusern	familienweise	zusammen;	der	zweite
their	houses	family-wise	together	the	second

Abschnitt	des	Weihnachtsabends	hatte	begonnen.
part	of the	christmas evening	had	begun

Als	Reinhard	in	die	Nähe	des	Ratskellers	kam,	hörte
When	Reinhard	in	the	vicinity	of the	council-cellar (pub)	came	heard

er	aus	der	Tiefe	herauf	Geigenstrich	und	den	Gesang
he	from	the	depth	up	violin play	and	the	singing

des	Zithermädchens;	nun	klingelte	unten	die	Kellertür,
of the	zither girl	now	rang	under	the	cellar door

und	eine	dunkle	Gestalt	schwankte	die	breite,	matt
and	a	dark	shape	swayed	the	wide	dim

erleuchtete	Treppe	herauf.
lit	stairs	up

Reinhard trat in den Häuserschatten und ging
Reinhard stepped in(to) the shadows of the houses and went

dann rasch vorüber. Nach einer Weile erreichte er den
then quickly past After a while reached he the

erleuchteten Laden eines Juweliers, und nachdem er
lit shop of a jeweler and after he

hier ein kleines Kreuz mit roten Korallen eingehandelt
here a small cross with red corals in-dealt
(bought)

hatte, ging er auf demselben Wege, den er gekommen
had went he on the same road that he come

war, wieder zurück.
was again back

Nicht weit von seiner Wohnung bemerkte er ein
Not far from his house noticed he a

kleines, in klägliche Lumpen gehülltes Mädchen an einer
little in miserable rags dressed girl at a

hohen Haustür stehen, in vergeblicher Bemühung, sie
high house-door stand in vain effort her

zu öffnen.
to open

"Soll ich dir helfen?" sagte er.
Shall I you help said he

Das	Kind	erwiderte	nichts,	ließ	aber	die	schwere
The	child	ansered	nothing	let	however	the	heavy

Türklinke	fahren.	Reinhard	hatte	schon	die	Tür	geöffnet.
door handle	go	Reinhard	had	already	the	door	opened

"Nein,"	sagte	er,	"sie	könnten	dich	hinausjagen;	komm
No	said	he	they	can	you	chase out	come

mit	mir!	ich	will	dir	Weihnachtskuchen	geben."
with	me	I	shall	you	christmas cake	give

Dann	machte	er	die	Tür	wieder	zu	und	faßte	das
Then	made	he	the	door	again	to	and	grabbed	the

closed he the door again

kleine	Mädchen	an	der	Hand,	das	stillschweigend	mit
little	girl	by	the	hand	that (who)	in silence	with

ihm	in	seine	Wohnung	ging.
him	in	his	house	went

Er	hatte	das	Licht	beim	Weggehen	brennen	lassen.
He	had	the	light	at the	away going	burn	let

when leaving

"Hier	hast	du	Kuchen,"	sagte	er	und	gab	ihr	die
Here	have	you	cake	said	he	and	gave	her	the

Hälfte	seines	ganzen	Schatzes	in	ihre	Schürze,	nur
half	of his	total	treasure	in	her	apron	only

keine	mit	den	Zuckerbuchstaben.
none	with	the	sugar letters

"Nun geh nach Haus und gib deiner Mutter auch
Now go to house and give your mother also

davon."
there from

Das Kind sah mit einem scheuen Blick zu ihm
The child looked with a shy look at him

hinauf; es schien solcher Freundlichkeit ungewohnt und
up it seemed such friendliness unused and

nichts darauf erwidern zu können. Reinhard machte die
not there-on answer to be able Reinhard made the

Tür auf und leuchtete ihr, und nun flog die Kleine
door up and lit (the way) (for) her and now flew the little one
(open)

wie ein Vogel mit ihrem Kuchen die Treppe hinab und
as a bird with her cake the stairs down and

zum Hause hinaus.
to the house out
out of the house

Reinhard schürte das Feuer in seinem Ofen an und
Reinhard poked the fire in his oven on and

stellte das bestaubte Tintenfaß auf seinen Tisch; dann
set the dusty ink holder on his table then

setzte er sich hin und schrieb und schrieb die ganze
set he himself to and wrote and wrote the whole

Nacht Briefe an seine Mutter, an Elisabeth.
night letters to his mother to Elisabeth

Der	Rest	der	Weihnachtskuchen	lag	unberührt	neben
The	rest	of the	christmas cake	lay	ontouched	next to

ihm;	aber	die	Manschetten	von	Elisabeth	hatte	er
him	but	the	cuffs	from	Elisabeth	had	he

angeknöpft,	was	sich	gar	wunderlich	zu	seinem	weißen
buttoned on	what (which)	itself	quite	strange	to	his	white

Flauschrock	ausnahm.	So	saß	er	noch,	als	die
fleece coat	out-took (stood out)	So	sat	he	still	as	the

Wintersonne	auf	die	gefrorenen	Fensterscheiben	fiel	und
winter sun	on	the	frozen	window panes	fell	and

ihm	gegenüber	im	Spiegel	ein	blasses,	ernstes	Antlitz
him	opposite	in the	mirror	a	pale	serious	face

zeigte.
showed

Daheim

Daheim
There-home
(At home)

Als	es	Ostern	geworden	war,	reiste	Reinhard	in	die
As	it	Easter	became	was	traveled	Reinhard	in	the

Heimat.	Am	Morgen	nach	seiner	Ankunft	ging	er	zu
motherland	At the	morning	after	his	arrival	went	he	to

Elisabeth.
Elisabeth

"Wie	groß	du	geworden	bist,"	sagte	er,	als	das
How	big	you	become	are	said	he	as	the

schöne,	schmächtige	Mädchen	ihm	lächelnd	entgegenkam.
beautiful	slender	girl	him	smiling	against came (came to meet)

Sie	errötete,	aber	sie	erwiderte	nichts;	ihre	Hand,	die
She	blushed	but	she	answered	nothing	her	hand	that

er	beim	Willkommen	in	die	seine	genommen,	suchte
he	by the	welcoming	in	the	his	taken (had)	searched (tried)

sie	ihm	sanft	zu	entziehen.	Er	sah	sie	zweifelnd	an,
she	him	softly	to	pull away	He	looked	her	hesitating	on
								looked at her hesitatingly	

das	hatte	sie	früher	nicht	getan;	nun	war	es,	als
that	had	she	earlier (before)	not	done	now	was	it	as

trete	etwas	Fremdes	zwischen	sie.
stepped	something	foreign	between	them

Das blieb auch, als er schon länger dagewesen, und
That remained also when he already longer there-been and
(had been there)

als er Tag für Tag immer wiedergekommen war. Wenn
when he day for day always back come was When
(by)

sie allein zusammensaßen, entstanden Pausen, die ihm
they alone together sat arose pauses that him

peinlich waren, und denen er dann ängstlich
painful were and which he then fearfully
(anxiously)

zuvorzukommen suchte. Um während der Ferienzeit eine
before-come searched For during the vacation-time a
tried to avoid

bestimmte Unterhaltung zu haben, fing er an,
certain entertainment to have caught he on
started he

Elisabeth in der Botanik zu unterrichten, womit er
Elisabeth in the botany to teach where-with he
(with which)

sich in den ersten Monaten seines Universitätslebens
himself in the first months of his university life

angelegentlich beschäftigt hatte.
insistently busied had

Elisabeth, die ihm in allem zu folgen gewohnt und
Elisabeth who him in all to follow used and

überdies lehrhaft war, ging bereitwillig darauf ein. Nun
over-this instructive was went voluntarily there-on in Now
(moreover) liked to learn with it

wurden mehrere Male in der Woche Exkursionen ins
became multiple times in the week excursions in the

Feld oder in die Heide gemacht, und hatten sie dann
field or in the heath made and had they then

56

mittags	die	grüne	Botanisierkapsel	voll	Kraut	und
in the afternoon	the	green	botany container	full	(of) herbs	and

Blumen	nach	Hause	gebracht,	so	kam	Reinhard
flowers	to	(the) house	brought	so (then)	came	Reinhard

einige	Stunden	später	wieder,	um	mit	Elisabeth	den
some	hours	later	again	for	with	Elisabeth	the

gemeinschaftlichen	Fund	zu	teilen.
communal (their both's)	find	to	share

In	solcher	Absicht	trat	er	eines	Nachmittags	ins
In such / With such	such	intention	stepped	he	one	afternoon	in the

Zimmer,	als	Elisabeth	am	Fenster	stand	und	ein
room	as	Elisabeth	an the	window	stood	and	a

vergoldetes	Vogelbauer,	das	er	sonst	dort	nicht	gesehen,
gilded	birdcage	that	he	usually (before)	there	not	seen (had)

mit	frischem	Hühnerschwarm	besteckte.	Im	Bauer
with	fresh	chicken swarm (little plants that chickens like)	covered	In the	cage

saß	ein	Kanarienvogel,	der	mit	den	Flügeln	schlug
sat	a	canary bird	which	with	the	wings	beat

und	kreischend	nach	Elisabeths	Finger	pickte.	Sonst
and	screaming (shrill cries)	after	Elisabeth's	finger	nabbed	Usually (Before)

hatte	Reinhards	Vogel	an	dieser	Stelle	gehangen.
had	Reinhard's	bird	at	this	spot	hung

57

"Hat mein armer Hänfling sich nach seinem Tode in
Had my poor Linnet itself after its death in

einen Goldfinken verwandelt?" fragte er heiter.
a goldfinch changed asked he cheerfully

"Das pflegen die Hänflinge nicht," sagte die Mutter,
That use to do the Linnets not said the mother

welche spinnend im Lehnstuhl saß. "Ihr Freund Erich
who spinning in the lean chair sat Your friend Eric
(armchair)

hat ihn heut' Mittag für Elisabeth von seinem Hofe
hat it today afternoon for Elisabeth from his farm

hereingeschickt."
here sent

"Von welchem Hofe?"
From which farm

"Das wissen Sie nicht?"
That know you not

"Was denn?"
What then

"Daß Erich seit einem Monat den zweiten Hof seines
That Eric since one month the second farm of his

Vaters am Immensee angetreten hat?"
father on the Immensee on-stepped had
(taken up)

"Aber Sie haben mir kein Wort davon gesagt."
But you have me no word there-from told

"Ei," sagte die Mutter, "Sie haben sich auch noch
Eh said the mother You have yourself also not

mit keinem Worte nach Ihrem Freunde erkundigt. Er
with no word after your friend informed He

ist ein gar lieber, verständiger junger Mann."
is a very dear sensible young man

Die Mutter ging hinaus, um den Kaffee zu besorgen;
The mother went out for the coffee to take care of
(get)

Elisabeth hatte Reinhard den Rücken zugewandt und
Elisabeth had Reinhard the back turned to and

war noch mit dem Bau ihrer kleinen Laube
was still with the construction of her little arbor

beschäftigt.
busied

"Bitte, nur ein kleines Weilchen," sagte sie; "gleich bin
Please only a little while said she soon am

ich fertig."
I done

Da Reinhard wider seine Gewohnheit nicht antwortete,
Then Reinhard against his habits not answered
(When)

so wandte sie sich um. In seinen Augen lag ein
so turned she herself around In his eyes lay a
(then)

plötzlicher Ausdruck von Kummer, den sie nie
sudden expression of sorrow which she not
(never before)

darin gewahrt hatte.
there-in observed had

"Was fehlt dir, Reinhard?" fragte sie, indem sie
What is wrong (with) you Reinhard asked she while she

nahe zu ihm trat.
close(r) to him stepped

"Mir?" sagte er gedankenlos und ließ seine Augen
Me said he thoughtless and let his eyes

träumerisch in den ihren ruhen.
dreamily in the hers rest

60

"Du siehst so traurig aus."
You see so sad out
You look so sad

"Elisabeth," sagte er, "ich kann den gelben Vogel nicht
Elisabeth said he I can the yellow bird not

leiden."
suffer

Sie sah ihn staunend an, sie verstand ihn nicht. "Du
She looked him amazed at she understood him not You
She looked surprised at him

bist so sonderbar," sagte sie.
are so strange said she

Er nahm ihre beiden Hände, die sie ruhig in den
He took her both hands which she calmly in the

seinen ließ. Bald trat die Mutter wieder herein. Nach
hers let Soon stepped the mother again inside After

dem Kaffee setzte diese sich an ihr Spinnrad;
the coffee set this one herself to her spinning wheel

Reinhard und Elisabeth gingen ins Nebenzimmer, um
Reinhard and Elisabeth went into the side room for

ihre Pflanzen zu ordnen.
their plants to order

61

Nun	wurden	Staubfäden	gezählt,	Blätter	und	Blüten
Now	became	dust threads (stamens)	counted	leaves	and	flowers

sorgfältig	ausgebreitet	und	von	jeder	Art	zwei
carefully	opened	and	from	each	sort	two

Exemplare	zum	Trocknen	zwischen	die	Blätter	eines
exemplars	to the (for)	drying	between	the	leaves	of a

großen	Folianten	gelegt.
large	tome	laid

Es	war	sonnige	Nachmittagsstille;	nur	nebenan	schnurrte
It	was	(a) sunny	afternoon's quiet	only	next-to (to the side)	zoomed

der	Mutter	Spinnrad,	und	von	Zeit	zu	Zeit	wurde
the	mother('s)	spinning wheel	and	from	time	to	time	became (was)

Reinhards	gedämpfte	Stimme	gehört,	wenn	er	die
Reinhard's	dampened (muted)	voice	heard	when	he	the

Ordnungen	der	Klassen	der	Pflanzen	nannte	oder
orders	of the	classes	of the	plants	named	or

Elisabeths	ungeschickte	Aussprache	der	lateinischen
Elisabeth's	incorrect	pronunciation	of the	Latin

Namen	korrigierte.
name	corrected

"Mir fehlt noch von neulich die Maiblume," sagte
Me (it) lacks still from the other day the May-flower said

sie jetzt, als der ganze Fund bestimmt und geordnet
she now as the whole find identified and ordened

war.
was

Reinhard zog einen kleinen weißen Pergamentband aus
Reinhard pulled a small white parchment band from
(vellum)

der Tasche. "Hier ist ein Maiblumenstengel für dich,"
the pocket Here is a May-flower for you

sagte er, indem er die halbgetrocknete Pflanze
said he while he the half dried plant

herausnahm.
out took

Als Elisabeth die beschriebenen Blätter sah, fragte sie:
As Elisabeth the written on leaves saw asked she

"Hast du wieder Märchen gedichtet?"
Have you again fairy tales composed

"Es sind keine Märchen," antwortete er und reichte ihr
It are no fairy tales answered he and reached her
(They) (handed)

das Buch.
the book

63

Es waren lauter Verse, die meisten füllten höchstens
It were only verses the most filled at most

eine Seite. Elisabeth wandte ein Blatt nach dem andern
one side Elisabeth turned one leaf after the others
(page)

um; sie schien nur die Überschriften zu lesen. "Als
around she seemed only the titles to read When

sie vom Schulmeister gescholten war." "Als sie
she by the school master scolded was When they

sich im Walde verirrt hatten." "Mit dem
themselves in the forest lost had With the

Ostermärchen." "Als sie mir zum erstenmal geschrieben
Easter fairy tales When she me for the first time written

hatte;" in der Weise lauteten fast alle.
had in that manner sounded almost all

Reinhard blickte forschend zu ihr hin, und indem sie
Reinhard glanced searchingly to her over and while she

immer weiter blätterte, sah er, wie zuletzt auf ihrem
always further leafed saw he how at last on her

klaren Antlitz ein zartes Rot hervorbrach und es
clear face a delicate read broke out and it

allmählich ganz überzog. Er wollte ihre Augen sehen,
gradually totally drew over He wanted her eyes see
(covered)

aber Elisabeth sah nicht auf und legte das Buch am
but Elisabeth saw not up and put the book to the

Ende schweigend vor ihn hin.
end in silence before him away

"Gib mir es nicht so zurück!" sagte er.
Give me it not thus back said he
(like that)

Sie nahm ein braunes Reis aus der Blechkapsel. "Ich
She took a brown twig from the tin case I

will dein Lieblingskraut hineinlegen," sagte sie und gab
shall your favorite herb lay in said she and gave

ihm das Buch in seine Hände.
him the book in his hands

Endlich kam der letzte Tag der Ferienzeit und der
Finally came the last day of the vacations-time and the

Morgen der Abreise. Auf ihre Bitte erhielt Elisabeth
morning of the departure On her request became Elisabeth

von der Mutter die Erlaubnis, ihren Freund an den
from the mother the permission her friend to the

Postwagen zu begleiten, der einige Straßen von ihrer
postal coach to escort which some streets from their

Wohnung seine Station hatte.
house its station had

Als sie vor die Haustür traten, gab Reinhard ihr
When they before the house door stepped gave Reinhard her
(out of)

den Arm; so ging er schweigend
the arm so went he in silence

65

neben	dem	schlanken	Mädchen	Je	näher	sie
next to	the	slender	girl	The	closer	they

her.
~~here~~
next to the slender girl

ihrem	Ziele	kamen,	desto	mehr	war	es	ihm,	er	habe
to their	target	came	the	more	was	it	him	he	have (had)

ihr,	ehe	er	auf	so	lange	Abschied	nehme,	etwas
her	before	he	on (for)	such	long	goodbye	take	something

Notwendiges	mitzuteilen,	etwas,	wovon	aller	Wert
necessary (important)	with-to-share (to tell)	something	where-from	all	worth

und	alle	Lieblichkeit	seines	künftigen	Lebens	abhänge,
and	all	loveliness (the love)	of his	future	life	depend

und	doch	konnte	er	sich	des	erlösenden	Wortes	nicht
and	still	could	he	himself	the	solving (right)	words	not

bewußt	werden.	Das	ängstigte	ihn;	er	ging
aware	become	That	frightened	him	he	went

immer	langsamer.
always	slower

slower and slower

"Du	kommst	zu	spät,"	sagte	sie,	"es	hat	schon	zehn
You	(will) come	too	late	said	she	it	has	already	ten

geschlagen	auf	St.	Marien."
struck	on	Saint	Marien (church tower)

Er	ging	aber	darum	nicht	schneller.	Endlich	sagte	er
He	went	however	there-for	not	faster	Finally	said	he

stammelnd:
stammering

"Elisabeth, du wirst mich nun in zwei Jahren gar
Elisabeth you will me now in two years at all

nicht sehen, wirst du mich wohl noch eben so lieb
not see will you my well still as such dear

haben wie jetzt, wenn ich wieder da bin?"
have as now when I again there am

Sie nickte und sah ihm freundlich ins Gesicht.
She nodded and looked him friendly in the face

"Ich habe dich auch verteidigt;" sagte sie nach einer
I have you also defended said she after a

Pause.
pause

"Mich? Gegen wen hattest du es nötig?"
Me Against who had you it necessary
was that

"Gegen meine Mutter. Wir sprachen gestern abend, als
Against my mother We spoke yesterday evening when

du weggegangen warst, noch lange über dich. Sie
you away gone were still long about you She

meinte, du seiest nicht mehr so gut, wie du
meant you are not (any)more so good as you

gewesen."
been (have)

67

Reinhard schwieg einen Augenblick; dann aber nahm
Reinhard kept silent (for) a moment then however took

er ihre Hand in die seine, und indem er ihr ernst
he her hand in the his and while he her seriously

in ihre Kinderaugen blickte, sagte er:
in her child's eyes looked said he

"Ich bin noch eben so gut, wie ich gewesen bin;
I am still as such good as I been am
(have)

glaube du das nur fest! Glaubst du es, Elisabeth?"
believe you that only fast Believe you it Elisabeth
(really)

"Ja," sagte sie.
Yes said she

Er ließ ihre Hand los und ging rasch mit ihr durch
He let her hand go and went quickly with her through

die letzte Straße. Je näher ihm der Abschied kam,
the last street The closer him the departure came

desto freudiger war sein Gesicht; er ging ihr fast
the more peaceful was his face he went her almost

zu schnell.
too fast

"Was hast du, Reinhard?" fragte sie.
What have you Reinhard asked she

"Ich habe ein Geheimnis, ein schönes!" sagte er und
I have a secret a beautiful (one) said he and

sah sie mit leuchtenden Augen "Wenn ich nach
looked her with shining eyes When I after
an.
at
looked at her with shining eyes

zwei Jahren wieder da bin, dann sollst du es
two years again there am then shall you it

erfahren."
hear

Mittlerweile hatten sie den Postwagen erreicht;
Meanwhile had they the postal coach reached

es war noch eben Zeit genug. Noch einmal nahm
it was still even time enough. Still once took
they still had

Reinhard ihre Hand. "Leb wohl!" sagte er, "leb wohl,
Reinhard her hand Live well said he live well

Elisabeth! Vergiß es nicht!"
Elisabeth Forget it not

Sie schüttelte mit dem Kopf. "Leb wohl!" sagte sie.
She shook with the head Live well said she

Reinhard stieg hinein, und die Pferde zogen an. Als
Reinhard rose in and the horses pulled on As
(climbed) started to pull

der Wagen um die Straßenecke rollte, sah er noch
the coach around the street corner rolled saw he still

einmal ihre liebe Gestalt, wie sie langsam den Weg
once her sweet shape as she slowly the road

zurückging.
back went

Ein Brief

Ein Brief
A letter

Fast zwei Jahre nachher saß Reinhard vor seiner
Almost two years after sat Reinhard before his

Lampe zwischen Büchern und Papieren in Erwartung
lamp between books and papers in awaiting

eines Freundes, mit welchem er
of a friend with whom he

gemeinschaftliche Studien Man kam die Treppe
communal studies One came the stairs
übte.
practiced
studied together

herauf. "Herein!" Es war die Wirtin. "Ein Brief für Sie,
up Here-in It was the landlady A letter for you
(Come in)

Herr Werner!" Dann entfernte sie sich wieder.
Sir Werner Then removed she herself again

Reinhard hatte seit seinem Besuch in der Heimat nicht
Reinhard had since his visit in the homeland not

an Elisabeth geschrieben und von ihr keinen Brief
to Elisabeth written and from her no letter

mehr erhalten. Auch dieser war nicht von ihr; es
(any)more become Also this was not from her it

war die Hand seiner Mutter.
was the hand of his mother

Reinhard brach und las, und bald las er folgendes:
Reinhard broke and read and soon read he (the) following
(opened)

"In Deinem Alter, mein liebes Kind, hat noch fast
In your age my dear child has indeed almost

jedes Jahr sein eigenes Gesicht: denn die Jugend läßt
each year its own face since the youth lets

sich nicht ärmer machen. Hier ist auch manches
itself not poorer make Here is also much

anders geworden, was Dir wohl erstan weh tun wird,
different become what you well first pain do will

wenn ich Dich sonst recht verstanden habe.
when I you before correctly understand have

"Erich hat sich gestern endlich das Jawort von
Eric has himself yesterday finally the Yes-word from

Elisabeth geholt, nachdem er in dem letzten Vierteljahr
Elisabeth fetched after that he in the last quarter year
(become)

zweimal vergebens angefragt hatte. Sie hatte sich
two times in vain requested had She had herself

immer nicht dazu entschließen können; nun hat sie es
always not there-to decided been able now has she it

endlich doch getan; sie ist auch noch gar zu jung.
finally indeed done she is also still quite too young

72

Die Hochzeit wird bald sein, und die Mutter wird
The wedding will soon be and the mother will

dann mit ihnen fortgehen."
then with them away go

Immensee

Immensee
Immensee

Wiederum	waren	Jahre	vorüber.	Auf	einem	abwärts
Again	were	years	past	On	a	down

führenden	schattigen	Waldwege	wanderte	an	einem
leading	shady	forest road	walked	on	a

warmen	Frühlingsnachmittage	ein	junger	Mann	mit
warm	spring-afternoon	a	young	man	with

kräftigem,	gebräuntem	Antlitz.
powerful	browned	face

a strong and tanned

Mit	seinen	ernsten	dunkeln	Augen	sah	er	gespannt	in
With	his	serious	dark	eyes	saw	he	anxiously	in

die	Ferne,	als	erwarte	er	endlich	eine	Veränderung
the	distance	as	expected	he	finally	a	change

des	einförmigen	Weges,	die	jedoch	immer	nicht
of the	uniform	road	which	however	always	not

eintreten	wollte.	Endlich	kam	ein	Karrenfuhrwerk
in-step (occur)	would	Finally	came	a	cart wagon (cart)

langsam	von	unten	herauf.
slowly	from	under	to up (up the hill)

"Hollah! guter Freund!" rief der Wanderer dem
Hi good friend called the walker the

nebengehenden Bauer zu, "geht's hier recht nach
along going farmer to goes it here straight to

Immensee?"
Immensee

"Immer gerad' aus," antwortete der Mann, und rückte
Always straight out answered the man and pulled

an seinem Rundhute.
on his round hat

"Hat's denn noch weit dahin?"
Has it then still far there to

"Der Herr ist dicht davor. Keine halbe Pfeif'
The gentleman is close there before No half (a) pipe

Tabak, so haben's den See; das Herrenhaus liegt hart
tobacco so has it the lake the manor lies close

daran."
there by

Der Bauer fuhr vorüber; der andere ging eiliger
The farmer drove past the other went more hurried

unter den Bäumen entlang. Nach einer Viertelstunde
under the trees along After a quarter hour

hörte	ihm	zur	Linken	plötzlich	der	Schatten	auf;
heard	him	to the	left	suddenly	the	shade	up
{aufhören; stop}	(he)						

der	Weg	führte	an	einen	Abhang,	aus	dem	die	Gipfel
the	road	led	to	a	clif	from	which	the	tops

hundertjähriger	Eichen	nur	kaum	hervorragten.
(of) hundred years old	oaks	only	just	reached up

Über	sie	hinweg	öffnete	sich	eine	weite,	sonnige
Over	them	away	opened	itself	a	wide	sunny

Landschaft.	Tief	unten	lag	der	See,	ruhig,	dunkelblau,
landscape	Deep	under	lay	the	lake	quiet	dark blue

fast	ringsum	von	grünen,	sonnenbeschienenen	Wäldern
almost	in a ring	by	green	sun lit	forests

umgeben;	nur	an	einer	Stelle	traten	sie
surrounded	only	on	one	spot	stepped	they
						(the forests)

auseinander	und	gewährten	eine	tiefe	Fernsicht,	bis
out (of) each other	and	presented	a	deep	far view	until
(apart)						

auch	diese	durch	blaue	Berge	geschlossen	wurde.
also	this	through	blue	mountains	closed	was
		(by)				

Quer	gegenüber,	mitten	in	dem	grünen	Laub	der
Straight	opposite	middle	in	the	green	foliage	of the
		in the middle of					

Wälder,	lag	es	wie	Schnee	darüber	her;	das	waren
forests	lay	it	as	snow	over	away	that	were

blühende	Obstbäume,	und	daraus	hervor	auf	dem
flowering	fruit trees	and	there from	before	on	the

hohen Ufer erhob sich das Herrenhaus, weiß mit roten
high shore raised itself the manor white with red

Ziegeln. Ein Storch flog vom Schornstein auf und
tiles A stork flew from the chimney up and

kreiste langsam über dem Wasser.
crossed slowly over the water

"Immensee!" rief der Wanderer.
Immensee called out the hiker

Es war fast, als hätte er jetzt das Ziel seiner Reise
It was almost as had he now the target of his journey

erreicht, denn er stand unbeweglich und sah über die
reached since he stood unmoving and looked over the

Gipfel der Bäume zu seinen Füßen hinüber ans
top of the trees to his feet over to the

andere Ufer, wo das Spiegelbild des Herrenhauses
other shore where the mirror image of the manor

leise schaukelnd auf dem Wasser schwamm. Dann
slow rocking on the water swam Then

setzte er plötzlich seinen Weg fort.
set he suddenly his way forth
{fortsetzen; continue}

Es ging jetzt fast steil den Berg hinab, so daß die
It went now almost steep the mountain down so that the

unten stehenden Bäume wieder Schatten gewährten,
under standing trees again shades presented

77

zugleich	aber	die	Aussicht	auf	den	See
at the same time	however	the	view	on	the	lake

verdeckten,	der	nur	zuweilen	zwischen	den	Lücken
hid	which	only	now and then	between	the	openings

der	Zweige	hindurchblitzte.
of the	branches	flashed through

Bald	ging	es	wieder	sanft	empor,	und	nun	verschwand
Soon	went	it	again	softly	up	and	now	disappeared

rechts	und	links	die	Holzung;	statt	dessen
to the right	and	to the left	the	woodland	instead	of that

streckten	sich	dichtbelaubte	Weinhügel	am	Wege
stretched	itself	close-foliaged (leafy)	wine hills	at the	road

entlang;	zu	beiden	Seiten	desselben	standen	blühende
along	to	both	sides	of the same	stood	flowering

Obstbäume	voll	summender	wühlender	Bienen.	Ein
fruit trees	full	(of) buzzing	burrowing	bees	A

stattlicher	Mann	in	braunem	Überrock	kam	dem
stately	man	in	brown	overcoat	came	the

Wanderer	entgegen.	Als	er	ihn	fast	erreicht	hatte,
walker	against (up to)	As	he	him	almost	reached	had

schwenkte	er	seine	Mütze	und	rief	mit	heller
swung	he	his	hat	and	called out	with	clear

Stimme:
voice

"Willkommen, willkommen, Bruder Reinhard! Willkommen
Welcome *welcome* *brother* *Reinhard* *Welcome*

auf Gut Immensee!"
on *(the) Estate* *(of) Immensee*

"Gott grüß' dich, Erich, und Dank für dein
God *greets* *you* *Eric* *and* *thanks* *for* *your*

Willkommen!" rief ihm der andere entgegen.
welcoming *called* *him* *the* *other* *against*

Dann waren sie zu einander gekommen und reichten
Then *were* *they* *to* *each other* *come* *and* *reached (shook)*

sich die Hände.
each other *the* *hands*

"Bist du es denn aber auch?" sagte Erich, als er so
Are *you* *it* *then* *but* *also* *said* *Eric* *as* *he* *so*

nahe in das ernste Gesicht seines alten Schulkameraden
close *in* *the* *serious* *face* *of his* *old* *school comrade*

sah.
looked

"Freilich bin ich's, Erich, und du bist es auch; nur
Freely am I it Eric and you are it too only
(Truly)

siehst du fast noch heiterer aus, als du schon
look you almost still more cheerful ~~out~~ as you already

sonst immer getan hast."
before always done have

Ein frohes Lächeln machte Erichs einfache Züge bei
A happy smiling made Eric's simple traits at

diesen Worten noch um vieles heiterer.
these words even for much more cheerful

"Ja, Bruder Reinhard," sagte er, diesem noch einmal
Yes brother Reinhard said he this one still once

seine Hand reichend, "ich habe aber auch seitdem
his hand reaching I have however also since then
(shaking)

das große Los gezogen; du weißt es ja."
the great lot pulled you know it yes
(fate)

Dann rieb er sich die Hände und rief vergnügt:
Then rubbed he himself the hands and called pleased

"Das wird eine Überraschung! Den erwartet sie nicht,
That will be a surprise That expects she not

in alle Ewigkeit nicht!"
in all eternity not

"Eine   Überraschung?"   fragte   Reinhard.   "Für   wen   denn?"
A   surprise   asked   Reinhard   For   whom then

"Für   Elisabeth."
For   Elisabeth

"Elisabeth!   Du   hast   ihr   nicht   von   meinem   Besuch
Elisabeth   You   have   her   not   from   my   visit

gesagt?"
told

"Kein   Wort,   Bruder   Reinhard;   sie   denkt   nicht   an   dich,
Not   (a) word brother   Reinhard   she   thinks   not   to   you
                                                                (of)

die   Mutter   auch   nicht.   Ich   hab'   dich   ganz   im
the   mother   also   not   I   have   you   wholly   in the

geheimen   verschrieben,   damit   die   Freude   desto   größer
secret   written   there-with   the   joy   the   greater

sei.   Du   weißt,   ich   hatte   immer   so   meine   stillen
be   You   know   I   had   always   so   my   silent

Plänchen."
little plans

Reinhard   wurde   nachdenklich;   der   Atem   schien   ihm
Reinhard   became   thoughtful   the   breath   seemed   him

schwer   zu   werden,   je   näher   sie   dem   Hofe   kamen.
heavy   to   become   the   closer   they   the   estate   came

81

An der linken Seite des Weges hörten nun auch
To the left side of the road heard now also
{aufhören; stop}

die Weingärten auf und machten einem weitläufigen
the wine gardens up and made a wide running
(expansive)

Küchengarten Platz, der sich bis fast an das Ufer
kitchen garden place that itself until almost to the shore

des Sees hinabzog. Der Storch hatte sich mittlerweile
of the lake down drew The stork had itself meanwhile

niedergelassen und spazierte gravitätisch zwischen den
down let and walked gravely between the

Gemüsebeeten umher.
vegetable beds around

"Hollah!" rief Erich, in die Hände klatschend, "stiehlt
Hey called Eric in the hands clapping steals

mir der hochbeinige Ägypter schon wieder meine kurzen
me the high-legged Egyptian already again my short
(long-legged)

Erbsenstangen!"
pea-sticks

Der Vogel erhob sich langsam und flog auf das Dach
The bird raised itself slowly and flew also the roof

eines neuen Gebäudes, das am Ende des
of a new building that at the end of the

Küchengartens lag und dessen Mauern mit
kitchen garden lay and whose walls with

82

| aufgebundenen | Pfirsich- | und | Aprikosenbäumen | überzweigt |
| bound up | peach | and | apricot trees | over branched |

| waren. |
| were |

| "Das | ist | die | Spritfabrik," | sagte | Erich; | "ich | habe | sie |
| That | is | the | spirit factory | said | Eric | I | have | her |

| erst | vor | zwei | Jahren | angelegt. | Die | Wirtschaftsgebäude |
| only | since | two | years | erected | The | farm buildings |

| hat | mein | seliger | Vater | neu | aussetzen | lassen; | das |
| has | my | blessed | father | newly | out-set (put up) | let | the |

| Wohnhaus | ist | schon | von | meinem | Großvater | gebaut |
| living house | is | already | by | my | grandfather | built |

| worden. | So | kommt | man | immer | ein | bißchen | weiter." |
| become | So | comes | one | always | a | bit | further |

| Sie | waren | bei | diesen | Worten | auf | einen | geräumigen |
| They | were | at | these | words | on | a | roomy (large) |

| Platz | gekommen, | der | an | den | Seiten | durch | die |
| place (yard) | come | which | on | the | sides | through (by) | the |

| ländlichen | Wirtschaftsgebäude, | im | Hintergrunde | durch |
| rural | farm buildings | in the | background | through |

| das | Herrenhaus | begrenzt | wurde, | an | dessen | beide |
| the | manor | limited | were | on | the which | both |

| Flügel | sich | eine | hohe | Gartenmauer | anschloß; | hinter |
| wings | itself | a | high | garden wall | locked to | behind |

83

dieser	sah	man	die	Züge	dunkler	Taxuswände	und	hin
this	saw	one	the	traits	(of) dark	yew tree walls (yew hedge)	and	to

und	wieder	ließen	Syringenbäume	ihre	blühenden	Zweige
and	back	let	lilac trees	their	flowering	branches

in	den	Hofraum	hinunterhängen.
in	the	farm space	down hang

Männer	mit	sonnen-	und	arbeitsheißen	Gesichtern	gingen
Men	with	sun	and	work-hot	faces	went

über	den	Platz	und	grüßten	die	Freunde,	während
over	the	yard	and	greeted	the	friends	while

Erich	dem	einen	oder	dem	andern	einen	Auftrag	oder
Eric	the	one	or	the	other	an	order	or

eine	Frage	über	ihr	Tagewerk	entgegenrief.
a	question	about	their	day work	towards called

Dann	hatten	sie	das	Haus	erreicht.	Ein	hoher,	kühler
Then	had	they	the	house	reached	A	high	cool

Hausflur	nahm	sie	auf,	an	dessen	Ende	sie	links	in
house floor	took	them	up	to	which	end	they	left	in

einen	etwas	dunkleren	Seitengang	einbogen.
a	somewhat	dark	side hallway	turned in

Hier	öffnete	Erich	eine	Tür,	und	sie	traten	in	einen
Here	opened	Eric	a	door	and	they	stepped	in	a

geräumigen	Gartensaal,	der	durch	das	Laubgedränge,
roomy (spacious)	garden saloon	which	through (because of)	the	crowding foliage

welches	die	gegenüberliegenden	Fenster	bedeckte,	zu
which	the	opposite lying	window	covered	to

beiden	Seiten	mit	grüner	Dämmerung	erfüllt	war;
both	sides	with	green	dusk	filled	was

zwischen	diesen	aber	ließen	zwei	hohe,	weit	geöffnete
between	these	however	let	two	high	wide	opened

Flügeltüren	den	vollen	Glanz	der	Frühlingssonne
wing doors	the	full	radiance	of the	spring sun

hereinfallen	und	gewährten	die	Aussicht	in	einen	Garten
fall in	and	presented	the	view	in	a	garden

mit	gezirkelten	Blumenbeeten	und	hohen	steilen
with	circled	flowerbeds	and	high	steep

Laubwänden,	geteilt	durch	einen	geraden,	breiten	Gang,
foliage walls	parted	by	a	straight	wide	walkway

durch	welchen	man	auf	den	See	und	weiter	auf	die
through	which	one	on	the	lake	and	farther	on	the

gegenüberliegenden	Wälder	hinaussah.
opposite lying	forests	saw out

Als	die	Freunde	hineintraten,	trug	die	Zugluft	ihnen
As	the	friends	stepped in	carried	the	draw-air (draft)	them

einen	Strom	von	Duft	entgegen.
a	flow	of	fragrance	towards

Auf	einer	Terrasse	vor	der	Gartentür	saß	eine	weiße,
On	a	terrace	before	the	garden door	sat	a	white

mädchenhafte	Frauengestalt.	Sie	stand	auf	und	ging	den
girl-like	female shape	She	stood	up	and	went	the

Eintretenden	entgegen;	auf	halbem	Wege	blieb	sie	wie
in stepping ones (people entering)	up to (to meet)	on	(the) half	way	remained	she	as

angewurzelt	stehen	und	starrte	den	Fremden
on-rooted (rooted)	stand	and	stared	the	stranger

unbeweglich	an.	Er	streckte	ihr	lächelnd	die	Hand
unmoving	on	He	reached	her	grinning	the	hand

entgegen.
~~against~~

"Reinhard!"	rief	sie,	"Reinhard!	Mein	Gott,	du	bist
Reinhard	exclaimed	she	Reinhard	My	god	you	are

es!	Wir	haben	uns	lange	nicht	gesehen."
it	We	have	us	long	not	seen
			not seen each other a long time			

"Lange	nicht,"	sagte	er	und	konnte	nichts	weiter	sagen;
Long	not	said	he	and	could	nothing	further (more)	say

denn	als	er	ihre	Stimme	hörte,	fühlte	er	einen	feinen
then	as	he	her	voice	heard	felt	he	a	delicate

körperlichen	Schmerz	am	Herzen,	und	wie	er	zu	ihr
bodily	pain	in the	heart	and	as	he	to	her

aufblickte,	stand	sie	vor	ihm,	dieselbe	leichte	zärtliche
looked up	stood	she	before	him	the same	light	tender

86

Gestalt, der er vor Jahren in seiner Vaterstadt
shape that he before years in his father-city
years ago

Lebewohl gesagt hatte.
live-well said had
(goodbye)

Erich war mit freudestrahlendem Antlitz an der Tür
Eric was with joy-beaming face by the door

zurückgeblieben.
back remained

"Nun, Elisabeth?" sagte er; "gelt! den hättest du
Now Elisabeth said he true that (one) had you

nicht erwartet, den in alle Ewigkeit nicht!"
not expected that (one) in all eternity not

Elisabeth sah ihn mit schwesterlichen Augen an.
Elisabeth looked (at) him with sisterly eyes at

"Du bist so gut, Erich!" sagte sie.
You are so good Eric said she

Er nahm ihre schmale Hand liebkosend in die seinen.
He took her small hand caressing in the his

"Und nun wir ihn haben," sagte er, "nun lassen wir
And now we him have said he now let we

ihn so bald nicht wieder los. Er ist so lange draußen
him so soon not again loose He is so long out there
(go) (has)

gewesen; wir wollen ihn wieder heimisch machen. Schau
been we want him again from home make Look

nur, wie fremd und vornehm aussehend er worden ist!"
only how strange and noble out-seeing he become is
(looking)

Ein scheuer Blick Elisabeths streifte Reinhards Antlitz.
A shy glance of Elisabeth streaked Reinhards face

"Es ist nur die Zeit, die wir nicht beisammen waren,"
It is only the time that we not together were

sagte er.
said he

In diesem Augenblick kam die Mutter, mit einem
In this moment came the mother, with a

Schlüsselkörbchen am Arm, zur Tür herein.
key little basket on the arm through the door in
(little basket)

"Herr Werner!" sagte sie, als sie Reinhard erblickte;
Sir Werner said she as she Reinhard saw

"ei, ein eben so lieber als unerwarteter Gast."
eh an equally so dear as unexpected guest

88

Und nun ging die Unterhaltung in Fragen und
And now went the conversation in questions and

Antworten ihren ebenen Tritt. Die Frauen setzten
answers their equal tread. The women set

sich zu ihrer Arbeit, und während Reinhard die für
themselves to their job, and while Reinhard the for

ihn bereiteten Erfrischungen genoß, hatte Erich seinen
him prepared refreshments enjoyed, had Eric his

soliden Meerschaumkopf angebrannt und saß dampfend
solid sea-foam-head burned and sat steaming
(pipe from light material)

und diskutierend an seiner Seite.
and discussing to his side.

Am andern Tage mußte Reinhard mit ihm hinaus auf
On the other day must Reinhard with him out on
(next)

die Äcker, in die Weinberge, in den Hopfengarten, in
the fields, in the wine hills, in the hop garden, in

die Spritfabrik. Es war alles wohl bestellt; die
the spirit factory. It was everything well ordered; the

Leute, welche auf dem Felde und bei den Kesseln
people, who on the field and at the kettles

arbeiteten, hatten alle ein gesundes und zufriedenes
worked, had all a healthy and satisfied

Aussehen.
look.

Zu Mittag kam die Familie im Gartensaal zusammen,
To afternoon came the family in the garden saloon together

und der Tag wurde dann, je nach der Muße der
and the day became then as to the trouble of the

Wirte, mehr oder minder gemeinschaftlich verlebt. Nur
host more or less communally spend Only

die Stunden vor dem Abendessen, wie die ersten des
the hours before the evening dinner as the first of the

Vormittags, blieb Reinhard arbeitend auf seinem
early afternoon remained Reinhard working on his

Zimmer.
room

Er hatte seit Jahren, wo er deren habhaft werden
He had since years where he them get hold become

konnte, die im Volke lebenden Reime und Lieder
could the in the people living rhymes and songs

gesammelt und ging nun daran, seinen Schatz zu
gathered and went now there-on his treasure to

ordnen und wo möglich mit neuen Aufzeichnungen
order and where possible with new notes

aus der Umgegend zu vermehren.
from the surroundings to increase

Elisabeth war zu allen Zeiten sanft und freundlich;
Elisabeth was to all times gentle and friendly

Erichs immer gleichbleibende Aufmerksamkeit nahm sie
Eric's always same remaining attention took she

mit einer fast demütigen Dankbarkeit auf, und
with an almost humble thankfullness up, and

Reinhard dachte mitunter, das heitere Kind von ehedem
Reinhard thought underwhile that cheerful child from before

habe wohl eine weniger stille Frau versprochen.
has well a less quiet woman promised
(would have)

Seit dem zweiten Tage seines Hierseins pflegte er
Since the second day of his here being used he

abends einen Spaziergang an den Ufern des Sees
in the evening a walk on the shore of the lake

zu machen. Der Weg führte hart unter dem Garten
to make. The road led hard under the garden
hard
(exactly)

vorbei. Am Ende desselben, auf einer vorspringenden
past. At the end of the same on a advanced
(of the garden)

Bastei, stand eine Bank unter hohen Birken; die Mutter
bastion stood a bench under high birches; the mother

hatte sie die Abendbank getauft, weil der Platz gegen
had it the evening bench baptised since the place towards

Abend lag und des Sonnenuntergangs halber um
(the) evening lay and of the setting sun half around

diese Zeit am meisten benutzt wurde.
this time to the most used became

Von	einem	Spaziergange	auf	diesem	Wege	kehrte
From	a	walk	on	this	road	turned

Reinhard	eines	Abends	zurück,	als	er	vom	Regen
Reinhard	one	evening	back	as	he	from	rain

überrascht	wurde.	Er	suchte	Schutz	unter	einer	am
surprised	became	He	searched	protection	under	a	by the

Wasser	stehenden	Linde,	aber	die	schweren	Tropfen
water	standing	Lime tree	but	the	heavy	drops

schlugen	bald	durch	die	Blätter.	Durchnäßt,	wie
struck	soon	through	the	leaves	Wet through and through	as

er	war,	ergab	er	sich	darein	und	setzte	langsam
he	was	gave	he	himself	therein	and	set	slowly

seinen	Rückweg	fort.
his	way back	on

Es	war	fast	dunkel;	der	Regen	fiel	immer	dichter.	Als
It	was	almost	dark	the	rain	fell	always	closer (more)	As

er	sich	der	Abendbank	näherte,	glaubte	er	zwischen
he	himself	the	evening bench	approached	believed	he	between

den	schimmernden	Birkenstämmen	eine	weiße
the	gleaming	birch trunks	a	white

Frauengestalt	zu	unterscheiden.	Sie	stand	unbeweglich
female shape	to	discern	She	stood	unmoving

und,	wie	er	beim	Näherkommen	zu	erkennen	meinte,
and	as	he	at the	approach	to	recognize	meant

zu	ihm	hingewandt,	als	wenn	sie	jemanden	erwarte.
to	him	turned	as	when	she	someone	expected

92

Er	glaubte,	es	sei	Elisabeth.	Als	er	aber	rascher
He	believed	it	were	Elisabeth	As	he	however	faster

zuschritt,	um	sie	zu	erreichen	und	dann	mit	ihr
to-stepped (approached)	for	her	to	reach	and	then	with	her

zusammen	durch	den	Garten	ins	Haus	zurückzukehren,
together	through	the	garden	in the	house	to return

wandte	sie	sich	langsam	ab	und	verschwand	in	den
turned	she	herself	slowly	away	and	disappeared	in	the

dunkeln	Seitengängen.
dark	side alleys

Er	konnte	das	nicht	reimen;	er	war	aber	fast	zornig
He	could	that	not	rhyme (place)	he	was	but (indeed)	almost	angry

auf	Elisabeth,	und	dennoch	zweifelte	er,	ob	sie	es
at	Elisabeth	and	still	doubted	he	whether	she	it

gewesen	sei;	aber	er	scheute	sich,	sie	darnach	zu
been	were	but	he	shied	himself	her	there-to	to

fragen;	ja,	er	ging	bei	seiner	Rückkehr	nicht	in	den
ask	yes	he	went	at	his	return	not	in	the

Gartensaal,	nur	um	Elisabeth	nicht	etwa	durch	die
garden saloon	only	for	Elisabeth	not	perhaps	through	the

Gartentür	hereintreten	zu	sehen.
garden door	step in	to	see

Meine Mutter Hat's Gewollt

Meine	Mutter	Hat's	Gewollt
My	mother	had it	wanted
			wanted it

Einige	Tage	nachher,	es	ging	schon	gegen	Abend,
Some	days	after	it	went	already	towards	(the) evening

saß	die	Familie,	wie	gewöhnlich	um	diese	Zeit,	im
sat	the	family	as	usual	around	this	time	in the

Gartensaal	zusammen.	Die	Türen	standen	offen;	die
garden saloon	together	The	doors	stand	open	the

Sonne	war	schon	hinter	den	Wäldern	jenseits	des
sun	was	already	behind	the	forests	on the other side	of the

Sees.
lake

Reinhard	wurde	um	die	Mitteilung	einiger	Volkslieder
Reinhard	became	for	the	sharing (telling)	of some	folk songs

gebeten,	welche	er	am	Nachmittage	von	einem	auf
asked	which	he	at the	afternoon	from (by)	one	on

dem	Lande	wohnenden	Freunde	geschickt	bekommen
the	land (countryside)	living	friends	send	become

hatte.	Er	ging	auf	sein	Zimmer	und	kam	gleich
had	He	went	on	his	room	and	came	immediately

darauf	mit	einer	Papierrolle	zurück,	welche	aus
there-on	with	a	paper roll	back	which	from

94

einzelnen sauber geschriebenen Blättern zu bestehen
single clean written pages to exist

schien.
seemed

Man setzte sich an den Tisch, Elisabeth an
One set themselves on the table Elisabeth to
(They)

Reinhards Seite. "Wir lesen auf gut Glück," sagte er,
Reinhards side We read on good luck said he
at random

"ich habe sie selber noch nicht durchgesehen."
I have her self still not through see
(read through)

Elisabeth rollte das Manuskript auf. "Hier sind Noten,"
Elisabeth rolled the manuscript up Here are notes

sagte sie, "das mußt du singen, Reinhard."
said she that must you sing Reinhard

Und dieser las nun zuerst einige tiroler
And this (one) read now first some from tirol

Schnaderhüpfel -dialektisch für "Schnitterhüpfen," d.
cutter-little hop dialect for cutter-little hop that

h. Schnitter-Tänze oder Lieder, die besonders in
means reaper dances or songs which mainly in

Tirol und in Bayern gesungen werden - indem er beim
Tirol and in Bayern sung are while he at the

Lesen zuweilen die lustige Melodie mit halber Stimme
reading occasionally the funny melody with half voice

anklingen ließ. Eine allgemeine Heiterkeit bemächtigte
sound let A general cheerfulness seized

sich der kleinen Gesellschaft. "Wer hat doch aber
itself of the small company Who has indeed however

die schönen Lieder gemacht?" fragte Elisabeth.
the beautiful songs made asked Elisabeth

"Ei," sagte Erich, "das hört man den Dingern schon
Eh said Eric that hears one the things already
                          can you hear of the things

an, Schneidergesellen und Friseure und derlei lustiges
on cutter apprentices and hair dressers and such funny

Gesindel."
riffraff

Reinhard sagte: "Sie werden gar nicht gemacht; sie
Reinhard said They were at all not made they

wachsen; sie fallen aus der Luft, sie fliegen über
grow they fall from the sky they fly over

Land wie Mariengarn - der Volksglaube hat dieses
land as Mary-weave the folk belief has this

feine Gewebe von Feldspinnen immer in Verbindung
delicate weave from field spiders always in connection

mit den Göttern gebracht. Nach Einführung des
with the gods brought After introduction of the

Christentums wurde es auf die Jungfrau Maria bezogen:
christianity became it on the maiden Maria drawn

aus dem feinsten Faden soll das Leichenkleid gewoben
from the finest weaves should the corpse dress woven

worden sein, worin Maria nach ihrem Tod eingehüllt
become be where in Maria after her death shrouded

wurde. Während ihrer Himmelfahrt wäre das Gewebe
became During her heaven ascension were the weave
(had)

wieder von ihr losgebrochen - hierhin und dorthin und
again from her loose broken here to and there to and

werden an tausend Stellen zugleich gesungen. Unser
were on thousand places at the same time sung Our

eigenstes Tun und Leiden finden wir in diesen Liedern;
very own doing and suffering find we in these songs

es ist, als ob wir alle an ihnen mitgeholfen hätten."
it is as if we all at them helped along had

Er nahm ein anderes Blatt: "Ich stand auf hohen
He took an other leaf I stand on high

Bergen..." (Ein altes Volkslied von einem schönen aber
mountains An old folk song from a beautiful but

armen Mädchen, das den jungen Grafen nicht heiraten
poor girl that the young count not marry

konnte, und sich in ein Kloster zurückzog.)
could and herself in a cloister withdrew

"Das kenne ich!" rief Elisabeth. "Stimme nur an,
That know I called Elisabeth Voice only on

Reinhard; ich will dir helfen."
Reinhard I want you help

Und nun sangen sie jene Melodie, die so rätselhaft
And now sang they that melody that so enigmatic

ist, daß man nicht glauben kann, sie sei von
is that one not believe can she is from
(by)

Menschen erdacht worden; Elisabeth mit ihrer etwas
people invented become Elisabeth with her somewhat

verdeckten Altstimme dem Tenor sekundierend.
hidden alt voice the tenor seconding

Die Mutter saß inzwischen emsig an ihrer Näherei;
The mother sat meanwhile industrious at her sewing

Erich hatte die Hände in einander gelegt und hörte
Eric had the hands in each other laid and listened

andächtig zu. Als das Lied zu Ende war, legte
attentive to As the song to end was lay

Reinhard das Blatt schweigend bei Seite. Vom Ufer
Reinhard the leaf in silence to (the) side From (the) shore

des Sees herauf kam durch die Abendstille das
of the lake up came through the evening silence the

Geläute der Herdenglocken; sie horchten unwillkürlich;
sound of the cowbells they hearkened unvoluntarily
(listened to it)

da hörten sie eine klare Knabenstimme singen:
then heard they a clear boy's voice sing

Ich stand auf hohen Bergen Und sah ins tiefe
I stand on high mountains And saw in the deep

Tal...
valley

Reinhard lächelte: "Hört ihr es wohl? So geht's von
Reinhard smiled Hear you it well So goes it from

Mund zu Mund."
mouth to mouth

"Es wird oft in dieser Gegend gesungen," sagte
It is often in this area sung said

Elisabeth.
Elisabeth

"Ja," sagte Erich, "es ist der Hirtenkasper; er treibt
Yes said Eric it is the shepherd joker he drives

die Färsen heim."
the heifers home

Sie	horchten	noch	eine	Weile,	bis	das	Geläute	hinter
They	listened to it	still	a	while	until	the	sound	behind

den	Wirtschaftsgebäuden	verschwunden	war.	"Das	sind
the	farm buildings	disappear	were (had)	That	are

Urtöne,"	sagte	Reinhard;	"sie	schlafen	in
ancient tones	said	Reinhard	they	sleep	in

Waldesgründen;	Gott	weiß,	wer	sie	gefunden	hat."
forest grounds	God	knows	who	them	found	has

Er	zog	ein	neues	Blatt	heraus.
He	pulled	a	new	leaf	out

Es	war	schon	dunkler	geworden;	ein	roter	Abendschein
It	was	already	dark	become	a	red	evening shine

lag	wie	Schaum	auf	den	Wäldern	jenseits	des
lay	as	foam	on	the	forests	on the other side	of the

Sees.	Reinhard	rollte	das	Blatt	auf,	Elisabeth	legte	an
lake	Reinhard	rolled	the	leaf	up (open)	Elisabeth	lay	at

der	einen	Seite	ihre	Hand	darauf	und	sah	mit
the	one	side	her	hand	there on	and	looked	along

hinein.	Dann	las	Reinhard:
inside	Then	read	Reinhard

Meine	Mutter	hat's	gewollt,
My	mother	had it	wanted

Den andern ich nehmen sollt':
The other I take should

Was ich zuvor besessen,
Were I before obsessed

Mein Herz sollt' es vergessen;
My heart should it forget

Das hat es nicht gewollt.
That has it not wanted

Meine Mutter klag' ich an,
My mother complain I on
I accuse

Sie hat nicht wohl getan;
She has not well done
honored

Was sonst in Ehren stünde,
What before in honor stood

Nun ist es worden Sünde.
Now is it become sin

Was fang' ich an!
What catch I on
What can I do

Für all' mein' Stolz und Freud'
For all my pride and happiness

Gewonnen hab' ich Leid.
Won have I suffering

Ach, wär' das nicht geschehen,
Ah were it not happened

Ach, könnt' ich betteln gehen
Ah could I begging go

Über die braune Heid'!
Over the brown heath

Während des Lesens hatte Reinhard ein unmerkliches
During the reading had Reinhard an imperceptible

Zittern des Papiers empfunden; als er zu Ende war,
trembling of the paper perceived; as he at (the) end was

schob Elisabeth leise ihren Stuhl zurück und ging
pushed Elisabeth slowly her chair back and went

schweigend in den Garten hinab. Ein Blick der Mutter
in silence   in   the   garden   down   A   glance   of the   mother

folgte ihr. Erich wollte nachgehen; doch die Mutter
followed   her   Eric   wanted   to go after   but   the   mother

sagte: "Elisabeth hat draußen zu tun." So
said   Elisabeth   has   outside   to   do (something)   So

unterblieb es.
remained under   it
was it ignored

Draußen aber legte sich der Abend mehr und mehr
Outside   however   laid   itself   the   evening   more   and   more

über Garten und See; die Nachtschmetterlinge schossen
over   garden   and   lake   the   night-butterflies (moths)   shot

surrend an den offenen Türen vorüber, durch welche
zooming   by   the   open   doors   past   through   which

der Duft der Blumen und Gesträuche immer stärker
the   fragrance   of the   flowers   and   shrubs   always   stronger

hereindrang; vom Wasser herauf kam das Geschrei
inside penetrated   from the   water   up   came   the   cry

der Frösche, unter den Fenstern schlug eine
of the   frogs   under   the   windows   struck (sounded)   a

Nachtigall, tiefer im Garten eine andere; der Mond
nightingale   deeper   in the   garden   an   other (one)   the   moon

sah über die Bäume.
looked   over   the   flowers

Reinhard blickte noch eine Weile auf die Stelle, wo
Reinhard looked still a while on the spot where

Elisabeths feine Gestalt zwischen den Laubgängen
Elisabeth's delicate shape between the foliaged walks

verschwunden war; dann rollte er sein Manuskript
disappeared was then rolled he his manuscript

zusammen, grüßte die Anwesenden und ging durchs
together greeted those present and went through the

Haus an das Wasser hinab.
house to the water down

Die Wälder standen schweigend und warfen ihr Dunkel
The forests stood in silence and threw their darkness

weit auf den See hinaus, während die Mitte desselben
far on the lake out while the middle of the same

in schwüler Mondesdämmerung lag. Mitunter
in sultry moon's twilight lay Middle under
(From time to time)

schauerte ein leises Säuseln durch die Bäume; aber es
shuddered a slight murmur through the trees but it

war kein Wind, es war nur das Atmen der
was no wind it was only the breathing of the

Sommernacht.
summer night

Reinhard	ging	immer	am	Ufer	entlang.		Einen
Reinhard	went	always	to the	shore	along		A

along the shore

Steinwurf	vom	Lande	konnte	er	eine	weiße
stone's throw	from the	land	could	he	a	white

Wasserlilie		erkennen.		Auf		einmal
water lily		recognize		At		once

wandelte	ihn	die	Lust	sie	in	der	Nähe	zu
walked	him	the	desire	her	in	the	closeness	to

from close up

an,
on

seized him the desire

sehen;	er	warf	seine	Kleider	ab	und	stieg	ins
see	he	threw	his	clothes	off	and	rose	into the

(descended)

Wasser.	Es	war	flach;	scharfe	Pflanzen	und	Steine
water	It	was	shallow	sharp	plants	and	stones

schnitten	ihn	an	den	Füßen,	und	er	kam	immer	nicht
kut	him	at	the	feet	and	he	came	always	not

in	die	zum	Schwimmen	nötige	Tiefe.
in	the	to the	swimming	necessary	depth

Dann	war	es	plötzlich	unter	ihm	weg,	die	Wasser
Then	was	it	suddenly	under	him	gone	the	waters

quirlten	über	ihm	zusammen,	und	es	dauerte	eine
swirled	over	him	together	and	it	took	a

Zeitlang,	ehe	er	wieder	auf	die	Oberfläche	kam.	Nun
while	before	he	again	on	the	surface	came	Now

regte	er	Hand	und	Fuß	und	schwamm	im	Kreise
moved	he	hand	and	foot	and	swam	in the	circle

umher, bis er sich bewußt geworden, von wo er
around until he himself conscious became from where he

hineingegangen war. Bald sah er auch die Lilie wieder;
went in was Soon saw he also the lily again

sie lag einsam zwischen den großen blanken Blättern.
she lay alone between the large bare leaves

Er schwamm langsam hinaus und hob mitunter die
He swam slowly out and lifted middle-under the
(from time to time)

Arme aus dem Wasser, daß die herabrieselnden
arms from the water (so) that the off-trickling

Tropfen im Mondlichte blitzten; aber es war, als ob
drops in the moonlight flashed but it was as if

die Entfernung zwischen ihm und der Blume dieselbe
the distance between him and the flower the same

bliebe; nur das Ufer lag, wenn er sich umblickte, in
remained only the shore lay when he himself looked around in
(looked back)

immer ungewisserem Dufte hinter ihm. Er gab
always (more) uncertain scent behind him He gave

indes sein Unternehmen nicht auf, sondern schwamm
meanwhile his enterprise not up however swam

rüstig in derselben Richtung fort.
calmly in the same direction forth

Endlich war er der Blume so nahe gekommen, daß er
Finally was he the flower so close come that he

die silbernen Blätter deutlich im Mondlicht
the silver leaves clearly in the moonlight

unterscheiden konnte; zugleich aber fühlte er sich
discern could at the same time however felt he himself

in einem Netze verstrickt, die glatten Stengel langten
in a net trapped the smooth stems reached

vom Grunde herauf und rankten sich an seine
from the bottom up and twined themselves to his

nackten Glieder.
naked limbs

Das unbekannte Wasser lag so schwarz um ihn her,
The unknown water lay so black around him away

hinter sich hörte er das Springen eines Fisches; es
behind himself heard he the jumping of a fish it

wurde ihm plötzlich so unheimlich in dem fremden
was him suddenly so eerie in the foreign

Elemente, daß er mit Gewalt das Gestrick der
element that he with violence the knitting of the
(tangle)

Pflanzen zerriß und in atemloser Hast
plants ripped and in breathless haste

dem Lande zuschwamm. Als er von hier auf den See
the land to-swam As he from here on the lake
towards land swam

zurückblickte, lag die Lilie wie zuvor fern und einsam
looked back   lay   the   lily   as   before   far   and   alone

über der dunklen Tiefe.
over   the   dark   depth

Er kleidete sich an und ging langsam nach Hause
He   dressed   himself   ~~on~~   and   went   slowly   to   house

zurück. Als er aus dem Garten in den Saal trat,
back   As   he   from   the   garden   in   the   saloon   stepped

fand er Erich und die Mutter in den Vorbereitungen
found   he   Eric   and   the   mother   in   the   preparations

einer kleinen Geschäftsreise, welche am andern Tage
of a   small   business trip   which   an the   next   day

vor sich gehen sollte.
for   itself   go   would
     would take place

"Wo sind Sie denn so spät in der Nacht gewesen?"
Where   are   you   then   so   late   in   the   night   been
     (have)

rief ihm die Mutter entgegen.
called   him   the   mother   towards

"Ich?" erwiderte er; "ich wollte die Wasserlilie besuchen;
I   answered   he   I   wanted   the   waterlily   visit

es ist aber nichts daraus geworden."
it   is   however   nothing   there from   become

"Das versteht wieder einmal kein sagte
That understands again once no said

Mensch!"
human

No one understands that

Erich. "Was Tausend hattest du denn mit der
Eric What thousand had you then with the

Wasserlilie zu tun?"
waterlily to do

"Ich habe sie früher einmal gekannt," sagte Reinhard;
I have her before once known said Reinhard

"es ist aber schon lange her."
it is however already long ago

Elisabeth

Elisabeth
Elisabeth

Am	folgenden	Nachmittag	wanderten	Reinhard	und
At the	following	afternoon	walked	Reinhard	and

Elisabeth	jenseits	des	Sees	bald	durch	die
Elisabeth	on the other side	of the	lake	soon (now)	through	the

Holzung,	bald	auf	dem	vorspringenden	Uferrande.
woodland	soon (now)	on	the	overhanging	shore edge

Elisabeth	hatte	von	Erich	den	Auftrag	erhalten,	während
Elisabeth	had	from	Eric	the	mission	become	during

seiner	und	der	Mutter	Abwesenheit	Reinhard	mit	den
his	and	the	mother's	absence	Reinhard	with	the

schönsten	Aussichten	der	nächsten	Umgegend,
most beautiful	views	from the	close	surrounding area

namentlich	von	der	andern	Uferseite	auf	den	Hof
namely	from	the	other	shore	on	the	manor

selber,	bekannt	zu	machen.	Nun	gingen	sie	von	einem
itself	familiar	to	make	Now	went	they	from	one

Punkt	zum	andern.
point	to the	other

Endlich wurde Elisabeth müde und setzte sich in den
Finally became Elisabeth tired and set herself in the

Schatten überhängender Zweige; Reinhard stand ihr
shade (of) overhanging branches Reinhard stood (of) her

gegenüber, an einen Baumstamm gelehnt; da hörte er
opposite to a tree trunk leant then heard he

tiefer im Walde den Kuckuck rufen, und es kam ihm
deeper in the forest the cuckoo call and it came him

plötzlich, dies alles sei schon einmal eben so gewesen.
suddenly this all were already once just so been
(had)

Er sah sie seltsam lächelnd an.
He looked her strangely smiling at

"Wollen wir Erdbeeren suchen?" fragte er.
Want we strawberries search asked he

"Es ist keine Erdbeerenzeit," sagte sie.
It is no strawberry time said she

"Sie wird aber bald kommen."
It will however soon come

Elisabeth schüttelte schweigend den Kopf; dann stand
Elisabeth shook in silence the head then stood

sie auf, und beide setzten ihre Wanderung fort; und
she up and both set their walk forth and
continued their walk

wie sie so an seiner Seite ging, wandte sein Blick
as she so by his side went turned his look
(like this)

sich immer wieder nach ihr hin; denn sie ging schön,
itself always again to her over since she went beautiful

als wenn sie von ihren Kleidern getragen würde. Er
as if she by her clothes carried was He

blieb oft unwillkürlich einen Schritt zurück, um sie
remained often unvoluntarily a step back for her

ganz und voll ins Auge fassen zu können.
all and full in the eye take to be able

So kamen sie an einen freien, heidebewachsenen Platz
So came they to a free heath-grown place

mit einer weit ins Land reichenden Aussicht. Reinhard
with a far in the land reaching view Reinhard

bückte sich und pflückte etwas von den am Boden
bent himself and picked something from the on the ground

wachsenden Kräutern. Als er wieder aufsah, trug sein
growing herbs As he again looked up bore his

Gesicht den Ausdruck leidenschaftlichen Schmerzes.
face the expression (of) passionate grief

"Kennst du diese Blume?" fragte er.
Know you this flower asked he

Sie sah ihn fragend an. "Es ist eine Erika. Ich
She looked him questioning at It is an Erika I

habe sie oft im Walde gepflückt."
have them often in the forest picked

"Ich habe zu Hause ein altes Buch," sagte er; "ich
I have at home an old book said he I

pflegte sonst allerlei Lieder und Reime
used always all kinds of songs and rhymes

hineinzuschreiben; es ist aber lange nicht mehr
to write in it is however long not (any)more

geschehen. Zwischen den Blättern liegt auch eine Erika;
happened Between the leaves lies also an Erika

aber es ist nur eine verwelkte. Weißt du, wer sie mir
but it is only a withered Know you who it me

gegeben hat?"
given has

Sie nickte stumm; aber sie schlug die Augen nieder
She nodded mutely but she struck the eyes down

und sah nur auf das Kraut, das er in der Hand
and looked only at the herb that he in the hand

hielt. So standen sie lange. Als sie die Augen gegen
held So stood they long As she the eyes towards

ihn aufschlug, sah er, daß sie voll Tränen waren.
him upstruck saw he that they full (of) tears were
(opened)

"Elisabeth," sagte er, "hinter jenen blauen Bergen liegt
Elisabeth said he behind those blue mountains lies

unsere Jugend. Wo ist sie geblieben?"
our youth Where is it remained
(has) (gone)

Sie sprachen nichts mehr; sie gingen stumm neben
They spoke not (any)more they went in silence next to

einander zum See hinab. Die Luft war schwül, im
each other to the lake down The air was sultry in the

Westen stieg schwarzes Gewölk auf. Es wird gewittern,"
West rose black clouding up It will thunderstorm

sagte Elisabeth, indem sie ihren Schritt beeilte;
said Elisabeth in that she her step hurried
(while)

Reinhard nickte schweigend, und beide gingen rasch
Reinhard nodded in silence and both went quickly

am Ufer entlang, bis sie ihren Kahn erreicht hatten.
on the shore along until they their boat reached had

Während der Überfahrt ließ Elisabeth ihre Hand auf
During the crossing let Elisabeth her hand on

dem Rande des Kahnes ruhen. Er blickte beim Rudern
the edge of the boat rest He looked at the rowing

zu ihr hinüber; sie aber sah an ihm vorbei in die
to her over she however looked to him past in the

Ferne. So glitt sein Blick herunter und blieb auf
distance So slid his gaze down and remained on

ihrer	Hand;	und	die	blasse	Hand	verriet	ihm,	was	ihr
her	hand	and	the	pale	hand	betrayed	him	what	her

Antlitz	ihm	verschwiegen	hatte.
face	him	not told	had

Er	sah	auf	ihr	jenen	feinen	Zug	geheimen	Schmerzes,
He	looked	on	it	this	delicate	trait	of secret	pain

der	sich	so	gern	schöner	Frauenhände	bemächtigt,
which	itself	so	eagerly	(of) beautiful	women's hands	masters

die	nachts	auf	krankem	Herzen	liegen.	Als	Elisabeth
which	at night	on	an ill	hart	lie	As	Elisabeth

sein	Auge	auf	ihrer	Hand	ruhen	fühlte,	ließ	sie	sie
his	eye	on	her	hand	rest	felt	let	she	it

langsam	über	Bord	ins	Wasser	gleiten.
slowly	over	(the) side	in the	water	slide

Auf	dem	Hofe	angekommen	trafen	sie	einen
On	the	farm	arrived	found	they	a

Scherenschleiferkarren	vor	dem	Herrenhause;	ein
scissors grinder	in front of	the	manor	a

Mann	mit	schwarzen,	niederhängenden	Locken	trat
man	with	black	down hanging	curls	stepped

emsig	das	Rad	und	summte	eine	Zigeunermelodie
industriously	the	wheel	and	hummed	a	gypsy melody

zwischen	den	Zähnen,	während	ein	eingeschirrter	Hund
between	the	teeth	while	a	harnessed	dog

schnaufend daneben lag. Auf dem Hausflur stand in
wheezing · there next · lay · On · the · house floor · stood · in

Lumpen gehüllt ein Mädchen mit verstörten schönen
rags · wrapped · a · girl · with · distraught · beautiful

Zügen und streckte bettelnd die Hand gegen Elisabeth
traits · and · extended · begging · the · hand · towards · Elisabeth

aus.
~~out~~

Reinhard griff in seine Tasche, aber Elisabeth kam
Reinhard · grasped · in · his · pocket · but · Elisabeth · came

ihm zuvor und schüttete hastig den ganzen Inhalt ihrer
him · before · and · shook · hastily · the · whole · content · of her

Börse in die offene Hand der Bettlerin. Dann wandte
purse · in · the · open · hand · of the · beggar girl · Then · turned

sie sich eilig ab, und Reinhard hörte, wie sie
she · herself · hurriedly · away · and · Reinhard · heard · how · she

schluchzend die Treppe hinaufging.
sobbing · the · stairs · up went

Er wollte sie aufhalten, aber er besann sich und
He · wanted · her · stop · but · he · re-thought · himself · and
He wanted to stop her · · changed his mind

blieb an der Treppe zurück. Das Mädchen stand
remained · on · the · stairs · back · The · girl · stood

noch immer auf dem Flur, unbeweglich, das empfangene
still always on the floor unmoving the received

Almosen in der Hand.
alms in the hand

"Was willst du noch?" fragte Reinhard.
What want you still asked Reinhard

Sie fuhr zusammen. "Ich will nichts mehr," sagte sie;
She moved together I want nothing more said she
       cringed

dann den Kopf nach ihm zurückwendend, ihn anstarrend
then the head to him back turning him staring at

mit den verirrten Augen, ging sie langsam gegen die
with the lost eyes went she slowly towards the

Tür. Er rief einen Namen aus, aber sie hörte es
door He called a name out but she heard it

nicht mehr; mit gesenktem Haupte, mit über der
not (any)more with sunken head with over the

Brust gekreuzten Armen schritt sie über den Hof
breast crossed arms walked she over the court

hinab:
away

Sterben, ach! sterben
Die ah die

Soll ich allein!
Must I alone

Ein altes Lied brauste ihm ins Ohr, der Atem
An old song roared him in the ear the breath

stand ihm still; eine kurze Weile, dann wandte er
stood him still a short while then turned he
stopped

sich ab und ging auf sein Zimmer.
himself away and went up his room

Er setzte sich hin, um zu arbeiten, aber er hatte
He set himself to for to work but he had

keine Gedanken. Nachdem er es eine Stunde lang
no thoughts After he it an hour long

vergebens versucht hatte, ging er ins Familienzimmer
in vain tried had went he in the family room

hinab. Es war niemand da, nur kühle grüne
down It was nobody there only cool green
(There)

Dämmerung; auf Elisabeths Nähtisch lag ein rotes
twilight on Elisabeths sewing table lay a red

Band, das sie am Nachmittag um den Hals
band that she on the afternoon around the neck

getragen hatte. Er nahm es in die Hand, aber es tat
worn had He took it in the hand but it made

ihm weh, und er legte es wieder hin.
him ache and he put it again away

Er hatte keine Ruhe, er ging an den See hinab und
He had no rest he went to the lake down and

band den Kahn los; er ruderte hinüber und ging noch
bound the boat loose he rowed over and went still
untied the boat

einmal alle Wege, die er kurz vorher mit Elisabeth
once all paths that he short before with Elisabeth

zusammen gegangen war. Als er wieder nach Hause
together went was As he again at home
(had)

kam, war es dunkel; auf dem Hofe begegnete ihm der
came was it dark on the yard met him the

Kutscher, der die Wagenpferde ins Gras bringen wollte;
coachman who the coach horses in the grass bring wanted

die Reisenden waren eben zurückgekehrt.
the traveling were just came back
(had)

Bei seinem Eintritt in den Hausflur hörte er Erich
At his entry in the house floor heard he Eric

im Gartensaal auf und ab schreiten. Er ging nicht
in the garden saloon up and down walk He went not

zu ihm hinein; er stand einen Augenblick still und
to him in he stand a moment still and

stieg dann leise die Treppe hinauf nach seinem
rose then slow the stairs up to his

Zimmer. Hier setzte er sich in den Lehnstuhl ans
room Here set he himself in the armchair at the

Fenster; er tat vor sich selbst, als wolle er die
window he did for himself self as wanted he the
pretended

119

Nachtigall hören, die unten in den Taxuswänden schlug;
nightingale hear that below in the yew hedges struck (sounded)

aber er hörte nur den Schlag seines eigenen Herzens.
but he heard only the beat(ing) of his own heart

Unter ihm im Hause ging alles zur Ruhe, die Nacht
Under him in the house went all to the rest the night

verrann, er fühlte es nicht.
went by he felt it not

So saß er stundenlang. Endlich stand er auf und legte
So sat he hours long Finally stood he up and lay

sich ins offene Fenster. Der Nachttau rieselte
himself in the open window the night dew trickled

zwischen den Blättern, die Nachtigall hatte aufgehört zu
between the leaves the nightingale had stopped to

schlagen. Allmählich wurde auch das tiefe Blau des
sound Gradually became also the deep blue from the

Nachthimmels vom Osten her durch einen blaßgelben
night heaven from the East away through a pale yellow

Schimmer verdrängt; ein frischer Wind erhob sich und
gleam pushed away a fresh wind rose itself and

streifte Reinhards heiße Stirne; die erste Lerche stieg
caressed Reinhards hot forehead the first lark rose

jauchzend in die Luft.
rejoicing in the air

Reinhard	kehrte	sich	plötzlich	um	und	trat	an
Reinhard	turned	himself	suddenly	around	and	stepped	to

den	Tisch:	er	tappte	nach	einem	Bleistift,	und	als	er
the	table	he	groped	after	a	pencil	and	as	he

diesen	gefunden,	setzte	er	sich	und	schrieb	damit
this	found	set	he	himself	and	wrote	there-with

einige	Zeilen	auf	einen	weißen	Bogen	Papier.	Nachdem
some	lines	on	a	white	sheet	(of) paper	After

er	hiermit	fertig	war,	nahm	er	Hut	und	Stock,	und
he	here-with	ready	was	took	he	hat	and	stick	and

das	Papier	zurücklassend	öffnete	er	behutsam	die	Tür
the	paper	back-leaving	opened	he	carefully	the	door

und	stieg	in	den	Flur	hinab.
and	rose (climbed)	in	the	floor	down

Die	Morgendämmerung	ruhte	noch	in	allen	Winkeln;	die
The	morning dawn	rested	still	in	all	corners	the

große	Hauskatze	dehnte	sich	auf	der	Strohmatte	und
large	house cat	stretched	itself	on	the	straw mat	and

sträubte	den	Rücken	gegen	seine	Hand,	die	er
ruffled	the	back	against	his	hand,	which	he

gedankenlos	entgegenhielt.	Draußen	im	Garten	aber
without thought	held towards (it)	Outside	in the	garden	however

sangen	schon	die	Sperlinge	großartig,	wie	Priester,	von
sang	already	the	sparrows	grand	as	priests	from

den Zweigen und sagten es allen, daß die Nacht
the branches and told it all that the night

vorbei sei.
over be

Da hörte er oben im Hause eine Tür gehen; es
Then heard he up in the house a door go it

kam die Treppe herunter, und als er aufsah, stand
came the stairs down and as he looked up stood

Elisabeth vor ihm. Sie legte die Hand auf seinen
Elisabeth before him. She put the hand on his

Arm, sie bewegte die Lippen, aber er hörte keine
arm, she moved the lips but he heard no

Worte.
words

"Du kommst nicht wieder," sagte sie endlich. "Ich weiß
You come not back said she finally I know

es, lüge nicht; du kommst nie wieder."
it lie not you come never back

"Nie," sagte er.
Never said he

Sie	ließ	ihre	Hand	sinken	und	sagte	nichts	mehr.	Er
She	let	her	hand	sink	and	said	nothing	(any)more	He

ging	über	den	Flur	der	Türe	zu;	dann	wandte	er
went	over	the	floor	the	door	towards	then	turned	he

sich	noch	einmal.	Sie	stand	bewegungslos	an
himself	still	once	She	stood	without moving	at

derselben	Stelle	und	sah	ihn	mit	toten	Augen	an.	Er
the same	spot	and	looked	him	with	dead	eyes	at	He

tat	einen	Schritt	vorwärts	und	streckte	die	Arme	nach
did	a	step	forwards	and	extended	the	arms	to

ihr	aus.	Dann	kehrte	er	sich	gewaltsam	ab	und
her	out	Then	turned	he	himself	violently	off (away)	and

ging	zur	Tür	hinaus.
went	to the	door	out

Draußen	lag	die	Welt	im	frischen	Morgenlichte,	die
Outside	lay	the	world	in the	fresh	morning light	the

Tauperlen,	die	in	den	Spinnengeweben	hingen,	blitzten
dew perls	which	in	the	spider webs	hung	flashed

in	den	ersten	Sonnenstrahlen.	Er	sah	nicht	rückwärts;
in	the	first	sun beams	He	saw	not	back

er	wanderte	rasch	hinaus;	und	mehr	und	mehr	versank
he	walked	quickly	out	and	more	and	more	sank

hinter	ihm	das	stille	Gehöft,	und	vor	ihm	auf	stieg
behind	him	the	silent	homestead	and	before	him	up	rose

die	große	weite	Welt.
the	great	wide	world

Wieder Der Alte

Wieder	Der	Alte
Again	The	Old (one)

Der	Mond	schien	nicht	mehr	in	die	Fensterscheiben;
The	moon	shone	not	(any)more	in	the	window panes

es	war	dunkel	geworden;	der	Alte	aber	saß	noch
it	was (had)	dark	become	the	old (one)	however	sat	still

immer	mit	gefalteten	Händen	in	seinem	Lehnstuhl	und
always	with	folded	hands	in	his	armchair	and

blickte	vor	sich	hin	in	den	Raum	des	Zimmers.
looked	before	himself	away	in	the	space	of the	room

Allmählich	verzog	sich	vor	seinen	Augen	die	schwarze
Gradually	pulled	itself	before	his	eyes	the	black

Dämmerung	um	ihn	her	zu	einem	breiten	dunkeln
dusk	around	him	away	to	a	wide	dark

See;	ein	schwarzes	Gewässer	legte	sich	hinter	das
lake	a	black	water	lay	itself	behind	the

andere,	immer	tiefer	und	ferner,	und	auf	dem	letzten,
other	always	deeper	and	deeper	and	on	the	last

so	fern,	daß	die	Augen	des	Alten	sie	kaum
so	far	that	the	eyes	of the	old (one)	it	hardly

124

erreichten, schwamm einsam zwischen breiten Blättern
reached swam alone between wide leaves

eine weiße Wasserlilie.
a white waterlily

Die Stubentür ging auf, und ein heller Lichtschimmer
The room door went open and a clear light gleam

fiel ins Zimmer.
fell inside the room

"Es ist gut, daß Sie kommen, Brigitte," sagte der
It is good that you come Brigitte said the

Alte. "Stellen Sie das Licht auf den Tisch!"
old (one) Put you the light on the table

Dann rückte er auch den Stuhl zum Tisch, nahm
Then moved he also the chair to the table took

eines der aufgeschlagenen Bücher und vertiefte sich
one of the opened books and immersed himself

in Studien, an denen er einst die Kraft seiner Jugend
in studies to which he once the power of his youth

geübt hatte.
practiced had

Made in the USA
Las Vegas, NV
18 December 2024

14615438R00080